Against Nature

This book questions the nature of the business and social information systems so ubiquitous in contemporary life. Linking positivism, individualism, and market-fundamentalist economics at the root of these systems, it critiques the philosophical ground of this triumvirate as fundamentally against nature. Connecting counter-philosophies of the subject as a natural part of existence, with more collectivist and ecological economics, it presents a historical critique of the development of the academic field of information systems and offers a complex view of the nature of Nature through which we might reshape our approach to technology and to our economies to overcome the existential threat of climate change. As such, it will appeal to philosophers, social theorists, and scholars of science and technology studies with interests in the environment and ecology, as well as those working in the field of information systems.

David Kreps is Reader in the Philosophy of Information Systems at the University of Salford, UK. His books include *Bergson, Complexity and Creative Emergence; Technology and Intimacy: Choice or Coercion;* and *Gramsci and Foucault: A Reassessment.*

Against Nature

The Metaphysics of Information Systems

David Kreps

LONDON AND NEW YORK

First published 2018 by Routledge

2 Park Square, Milton Park, Abingdon, Oxfordshire OX14 4RN
52 Vanderbilt Avenue, New York, NY 10017

Routledge is an imprint of the Taylor & Francis Group, an informa business

First issued in paperback 2020

British Library Cataloguing-in-Publication Data
A catalogue record for this book is available from the British Library

Library of Congress Cataloging-in-Publication Data
Names: Kreps, David, 1963– author.
Title: Against nature : the metaphysics of information systems / David Kreps.
Description: Abingdon, Oxon ; New York, NY : Routledge, 2018. | Includes bibliographical references and index.
Identifiers: LCCN 2018009448 | ISBN 9780815377757 (hbk) | ISBN 9781351233828 (ebk)
Subjects: LCSH: Information technology—Philosophy. | Computer science—Philosophy.
Classification: LCC QA76.167 .K74 2018 | DDC 004.01—dc23
LC record available at https://lccn.loc.gov/2018009448

ISBN: 978-0-8153-7775-7 (hbk)
ISBN: 978-0-367-60701-2 (pbk)

Typeset in Times New Roman
by Apex CoVantage, LLC

Contents

Tables

1 A transdisciplinary approach

This book offers a view on how to think about information systems if you want to engage with the philosophy of Green IT and Tech for Good. The positivist philosophy behind the information technology revolution is briefly unpacked and countered in this short polemic (I assume many readers will be familiar with much of this critique), and an alternative philosophy – process philosophy, as envisioned principally by Henri Bergson and Alfred North Whitehead – outlined that shines an entirely different light upon the nature of reality, and our place within it, and a way forward for the green-minded in the digital world.

As such, although in some ways situated within the academic field of Information Systems (IS), this is a transdisciplinary book. As IS scholars Dirk Hovorka and Jacqueline Corbett have said, 'IS is uniquely situated to transcend disciplinary boundaries, and rich research questions lie in the gaps between the traditional boundaries separating the business, humanities, and scientific disciplines.'[1] To a computer scientist, an information system is a piece of software. To a philosopher, the defining sum of all the discourse of a historical era – an 'episteme'[2] – is an information system. This book takes the latter view, digging up – with a nod to Michel Foucault's genealogical practice – the deep, discursive underpinnings that make IS possible, questioning them, and presenting countervailing arguments from the time when they arose.

You, the reader, therefore, will find philosophy – both metaphysical and political – economics, critical theory, complexity theory, ecology, sociology, contemporary investigative journalism, and much else besides, along with the signposts and reference texts of the Information Systems field. This is at once liberating for an author from the world of theatre who studied cultural theory and the sociology of technology whilst engaging as a coder in the early world of the Web and now teaches IS in a business school, studying philosophy in his spare time. It is also a challenge for any reader not familiar with a similar range of literature. 'Interdisciplinary books,' noted one philosopher of complexity, 'are notoriously problematic: sections that appear overly simplistic and old hat to one audience strike another as brand-new and difficult.'[3] My hope is that in the interconnections, arguments, and thrust of this polemic, readers will discover both interest and insight, alongside a range of new avenues to explore.

An additional challenge is that this is not a full-length monograph, with the space to spell out in detail many of the different angles that feed into the core argument. As such, it is inevitably selective and thereby – as is any selection – subjective. As a short polemic, it nonetheless allows me to focus upon the central claims:

- *that the early 20th-century philosophical grounding of today's digital revolution is culpable in digital's (growing) contribution to the ecological catastrophe unfolding in the 21st century*
- *that process philosophy offers a potential new way to rethink that philosophical grounding and to reshape the digital revolution to support strategies to counter that catastrophe*

As such, some readers may already see that not only, along with most technology studies scholars, do I assert that *technology is socially shaped,*[4] but that I question the commonly held 'instrumentalist' view of technology. This view suggests that technology itself is not inherently good or evil, but it is instead a neutral tool to be used or wielded. As celebrated technology ethicist Luciano Floridi has recently put it, such a 'dual-use' – for good or ill – approach to technology is both deceptive and inaccurate. 'The textbook example is the knife that can save a life or murder someone,' he says.

> And the trivial comment is that its use and hence moral evaluation depends on the circumstances. This is true, but insufficiently perceptive because not all knives are born equal. The very short, blunt and round knife that an airline provides to spread butter has a dual-use hugely oriented to fulfil a purpose that the butcher knife can also fulfil, but much less easily. A bayonet has a dual-use only theoretically because it is designed to kill a human being, not to cut the bread.[5]

My argument in this book is that the foundational philosophy underlying contemporary technology is not the neutral instrument the 'dual-use' view would have it be, but makes inscriptive and delimiting assumptions about the world and our place in it that are neither neutral nor good. This suggests that some innovations, or foundational assumptions, can act like the first word on a Scrabble board, determining what follows, until revolution or paradigm shift brings about a new game[6,7] An example of such 'technological enframement' is the alternating current (AC) electricity provided from a central source over a grid – so ubiquitous it takes a power cut for us to remember it – but which in fact determines the configuration of most of our electric devices; arguably a whole way of life. How different our societies might be if locally generated direct current (DC) electricity had always been the norm? That Edison's real innovation was the creation of the central power station,[8] and that he made a good deal of money out of this centralisation, is seldom remembered, and a salutary tale for those proponents of distributed local power generation on a roof-to-roof basis for whom such solar energy is a far cleaner and greener solution. Such enframement, whereby the parameters for each new innovation become more and more constrained as the board fills up, and the options for change become more and more contingent, can happen in the world of ideas, too – perhaps even more so.

Technologies can still be interpreted and used in different ways – there is *interpretive flexibility*[9] – and it remains within the power of individuals and groups to use technology for good, even if occasionally with some difficulty. But society is undoubtedly technologically shaped, too, and the socio-political context in which technology is developed, disseminated, adopted, and used today, and from which it springs, is geared towards using it not for good but for a particular evil: the continuing isolation of people from each other and from the natural world of which we ought to feel a part. This fundamental philosophical question – about just exactly what constitutes 'the good' and why we should pursue it – is the primary battleground in the ideas explored in this book: whether we are best alone or together.

From Information Systems as an academic field to today's digital revolution

Information Systems as an academic field lacks a strong self-concept and a coherent grounding philosophy. Loosely defined – by those closer to the computing than the socio-philosophical end of its spectrum – as the study and practice of placing computer technology in the context of its use, the field originated in the heat of the Second World War, applying the new computer science to operations management and organisation theory, evolving into a recognised field in the 1960s. Known variously as Management Information Systems (MIS) 'IT, IS, DSS, information management, information science, informatics,' – and, of course, more recently, the science behind the use and impact of information and communication technologies (ICTs), or, simply, 'digital', 'the whole Gestalt of the field remains elusive'[10] – not least, perhaps, because of the blurred boundaries with both computing and sociology. Rudy Hirschheim and Heinz Klein offered in 2012 a scholarly history of the field, which focussed upon 'a distinct academic, US-centric, business school-oriented, private sector focus, interpretive research method, systems development bias.'[11] Their story was of the evolution of the field, mostly in business schools and focussed mostly upon business systems, from the 1960s onward. In light of the current revolutionary changes in our societies, it is a story of how a sapling pushed its way up to establish itself in the world.

In today's societies, that sapling is rapidly becoming the giant tree that defines the entire ecosystem around it: 'digital transformation' as the current business buzz-term would have it, whereby the digitisation of various functions of organisations gives way to the complete reshaping of organisations for a digital society. Moreover, what used to be simply business machines, conceived in computing departments and created in computer corporations, with software conceived and often designed in business schools, are now handheld computing and communication devices at the heart of all our interpersonal relationships. Americans check their phones 8 billion times a day.[12] The 'digital footprints' of the children of Western societies begin with ultrasound scans on Facebook before they are born. In the villages in third world countries smartphones empower rural farmers with real-time commodity prices for their produce and up-to-date weather reports.[13] In advanced economies, we are already preparing for post-smartphone immersion in an always-on digital world, where tiny, discrete but connected machines lie ready to answer to every spoken request. Indeed, is any part of contemporary society not touched by the products of information systems practice? Known sometimes as 'digital innovation' or 'information technology,' labels which tame the power of information systems by containing them in manageable envelopes of understanding, the 'tech giants' (Apple, Facebook, Google, Microsoft, et al.) nonetheless have harnessed information systems to radically alter our lives, our economies, and our means of communication – with astonishing speed and unprecedented impact upon our societies and the environment. The coming 'fourth industrial revolution' promises to radically remake both us and the world around us.[14] Addressing the ontological and metaphysical bases of these changes, therefore, is of paramount importance.

In this book, then, looking back from this world of digital ubiquity, I am more interested in the philosophy and social context of the 1920s, 1930s, and 1940s – the soil in which the seeds of the Information Systems field took root. It is here that we find the foundational assumptions that – like the lines, pollinators, and pests of a hedgerow – have shaped the field ever since. It is here, in arguments at the time, that we can find alternative routes that might reshape the field. My suggestion in this book is that process philosophy, born in the late 19th/early 20th century, offers an ontological grounding through which we might newly understand – and change – this field.

Our relationship with nature

The sapling becoming the giant tree that defines the entire ecosystem around it turns out to be more of a yew than an oak. Oaks provide a rich and biodiverse habitat, hosting hundreds of species of insect, supplying birds with a key food source, and feeding mammals such as badgers and deer with acorns. Yew trees – *Taxus baccata* in Latin, from which we derive the word toxic – kill everything beneath them. So it is with digital transformation, as it sweeps away whole industries to put them in the pocket of the 'tech giants.' MacDonaldisation[15] turned into Uberisation.[16] More significantly, the underlying philosophy and much of its outcome runs counter to the health of the environment: it is *against nature.*

The core ecological crisis of our times boils down to three things:

- ***Energy***: the energy we use to power our 'fossil capitalism' societies (built around a central power station using carbon-based fuel) produces greenhouse gases that are warming the planet, causing what is popularly known as climate change, but coming to be described as 'climate breakdown'[17]
- ***Economic growth***: the production cycle of our economic growth model – how we make, use, and then discard things – is extremely inefficient, leading to massive and unsustainable resource depletion and enormous amounts of polluting waste
- ***Extinction***: the combination of climate change, and the twin impacts of resource depletion and pollution, are together responsible for what many are already calling the sixth great mass extinction of species on our planet – and our own species may well go with it[18]

The key role played by the products of information systems in this crisis boils down to:

- ***Energy***: energy use identifiably related to ICTs had reached parity with global air travel already in 2008[19] – before the smartphone revolution – and 'the electricity consumption and CO_2 emissions directly attributed to ICT devices and systems are soon expected to surpass the 10% and 5% marks respectively.'[20]
- ***Economic growth***: the production cycle of digital devices is immensely wasteful: over a billion iPhones have been made since 2007 using some 40 million tons of gold ore,[21] but the growth cycle promotes continual

upgrades, meaning each iPhone is used for only 18 months, and then discarded; approximately 50 million tons of eWaste are expected in 2018 with an annual 4% to 5% growth, and only 15% to 20% of all eWaste is recycled

- ***Extinction***: digital culture is urban, manufactured, hygienic, and social to an alienating extreme that makes us seemingly oblivious to the ongoing destruction of nature around us: the virtual distances us from the real

'The elite stance' of William Gibson's central character, Case, from the 1990s prophetic cyberpunk novel, *Neuromancer*, 'involved a certain relaxed contempt for the flesh. The body was meat.'[22] Cocooned in our contemporary digital ecosystems, we are largely unaware of the true impact of our lifestyles upon the natural world: the rural is nice in (home screen) pictures, but even our meat comes in carefully plastic-wrapped cartons. The big tech companies leading this digital culture meanwhile present themselves as platforms for personal liberation, whilst turning us into products in a zero-sum advertising industry where fake news, lies, and hate generate the most income.[23,24] The digital, in other words, is culpable in the ecological crisis of our day. For all that 'big oil' and other players may be more to blame for the origins and bulk of the problem,[25] the digital is both exacerbating the problem and, through mass distraction, delaying the changes needed to address it.

This book will not be focussing too greatly upon the issues of energy consumption, resource depletion, eWaste, and so on. These are for another work and other authors better versed in these problems. This book seeks out the philosophical foundations upon which information systems and today's digital culture bases itself, in order to challenge them, in the hope that the readers of this work may themselves challenge what they may contribute to when they engage in the field of information systems, science and technology studies, and related fields.

This book, therefore, questions the fundamental *nature* of the business and social information systems so ubiquitous in contemporary life. Linking the philosophy of positivism, the socio-political and methodological worldview of individualism, and market-fundamentalist economics at the root of these systems, it critiques the philosophical ground of this triumvirate as fundamentally *against nature*. Linking counter-philosophies of the human subject as a *natural* part of existence with collectivist and ecological economics, it presents a complex, monist, temporal view of the nature of Nature through which we might reshape our approach to technology and to our economies to overcome the existential threat of climate change.

It should be noted that much of the detail and argumentation included in the book is, perhaps inevitably, UK and US focussed. I – its author – am a British citizen, working within the UK HE sector, under the yoke of the Anglo-American model. I have great respect for Southern Theory,[26] and my philosophical approach is far more Continental – and French – than analytical. But I believe this focus is nonetheless appropriate, because the issues I am keen to critique are ones that are key to the Anglo-American model and need to be challenged.

In relating this argument, the book briefly recaps, in Chapter 2, a historical critique of the early development of the academic field of information systems, and thus the philosophical backdrop and approach of those engaged in creating the digital landscape we now inhabit. Focussing upon the philosophy of Logical Positivism at the root of such systems, it questions how these systems can be supportive of human social, emotional, and psychological needs when its core philosophy discounts their existence. It questions how our societies can creatively engage with the complex and delicate interdependencies of planetary ecology while we treat the natural as discrete and inert. It finds that a methodological individualism underpins this positivism – much to the detriment of our understanding of our environment.

The book, in Chapter 3, then draws upon process philosophy to argue for the reality of subjectivity – the nonphysical nature of subjective consciousness that is dependent upon but not determined by the physical nature of the body. It argues for a new concept of nature-on-the-move, as distinct from the bifurcation of nature that views only the objective – and static – as real. It presents arguments for a process-relational approach to understanding and building the information systems that increasingly run our societies. In Chapter 4, armed with this new philosophical standpoint, choices become clearer, between positivism and interpretivism, between an accent upon individualism or upon collectivism, and between reductionism and complexity. I introduce the notion of *systemic individualism* to help understand contemporary societies where inequality is at its worst. In Chapter 5, I present an outline of a second notion I introduce in this book, *infomateriality*, by which we might understand the true nature of the ubiquitous, always-on computational world information systems have brought about, and a call for a more collectivist ecological economics to be embedded within this infomateriality – before it is too late.

This book, therefore, couched within the academic field of Information Systems, is a piece of *critical* research from a philosophical standpoint. In its critique of the positivist approach to systems thinking, it links the political (methodological individualism), economic (market-led fundamentalism), and ecosystems (equilibrium ecology) approaches with the positivist approach to the creation of information technology artefacts in contemporary societies. It depicts these as all collectively rooted in a logical positivist denial of living, relational complexity. It counters this with a process approach to systems thinking, linking this to a political (collectivist), economic (ecological economics), and ecosystems (nonequilibrium ecology of complex adaptive systems) understanding of our environment and our place within its unfolding interconnectedness.

This book seeks to address the Information Systems community, and anyone interested in its foundations, and demands ontological clarity: *we need to be clear about what is real*. The ontological grounding of positivist approaches aligns with a methodological individualism of 'rational agents' (in computational market-fundamentalist economics) making them far more easily 'computable,' yet which depersonalizes, and indeed dehumanizes, the people for whom such systems are devised. Business and social information systems, in this sense, the more they are based in an ontological stand that divides object and subject are *inscriptive* of specific pliant and docile consumer identities. To use Foucault's term, we are disciplinated by such systems, and only to the benefit of those holding capital. This dehumanisation, moreover, inevitably plays into the disregard for natural ecosystems that characterises the manner in which we have, over the same period, poisoned our planet with the waste products of our consumption; the disregard for unverifiable values, moreover, renders bottom-line decision making unchallenged, while it is directly counter to the strategies required to combat climate change. In this manner, it turns out that our concept of nature – of what is real – is of existential importance.

'The ideas of economists and political philosophers, both when they are right and when they are wrong, are more powerful than is commonly understood,' wrote John Maynard Keynes.[27] It is my hope that, with a more process-relational philosophical outlook, embracing infomateriality as a true acknowledgement of our relationship with and impact upon our world, we may, through Tech for Green Good projects and a greater sense of responsibility in what we do, contribute, as IS scholars and practitioners, to a better world than the logic of our current trajectory unfortunately promises.

Notes

1 Hovorka, D.S., and Corbett, J. (2012) 'IS Sustainability Research: A Trans-Disciplinary Framework for a "Grand Challenge"' *33rd International Conference on Information Systems*. Orlando, FL.
2 Foucault, M. (1966/1997) *The Order of Things*. London: Routledge https://en.wikipedia.org/wiki/Episteme for a useful summary.
3 Juarrero, A. (2002) *Dynamics in Action: Intentional Behaviour as a Complex System*. London: MIT Press, p. 10.
4 Brey, P. (2003) 'Theorizing Technology and Modernity' in *Modernity and Technology*, Misa, T., Brey, P., and Feenberg, A. (eds.), pp. 33–71. Cambridge, MA: MIT Press.

5 Floridi, L. (2017) 'Infraethics – on the Conditions of Possibility of Morality' *Philosophy of Technology* 30(4), p. 392. Editor Letter https://doi.org/10.1007/s13347-017-0291-1
6 MacKenzie, D., and Wajcman, J. (eds.) (1992) *The Social Shaping of Society*. Cambridge, MA: MIT Press, p. 3.
7 Akrich, M., Callon, M., and Latour, B. (2002) 'The Key to Success in Innovation Part II: The Art of Choosing Good Spokespersons' Translated by A. Monaghan. *International Journal of Innovation Management* 6(2), pp. 207–225.
8 Hughes, T.P. (1983) *Networks of Power: Electrification in Western Society, 1880–1930*. Baltimore, MD: Johns Hopkins University Press, pp. 41–42.
9 Brey, P. (2003) 'Theorizing Technology and Modernity' in *Modernity and Technology*, Misa, T., Brey, P., and Feenberg, A. (eds.), pp. 33–71. Cambridge, MA: MIT Press.
10 Hirschheim, R., and Klein, H. (2012) 'A Glorious and Not-So-Short History of the Information Systems Field' *Journal of the Association for Information Systems* 13(4), p. 193.
11 ibid., p. 190.
12 Eadicicco, L. (2015) 'Americans Check Their Phones 8 Billion Times a Day' *Time Magazine* http://time.com/4147614/smartphone-usage-us-2015/
13 Beuermann, D.W., McKelvey, C., and Vakis, R. (2012) 'Mobile Phones and Economic Development in Rural Peru' *Journal of Development Studies* 48(11) (November 2), pp. 1–21 http://documents.worldbank.org/curated/en/308751468143976838/Mobile-phones-and-economic-development-in-rural-Peru
14 Schwab, K. (2016) *The Fourth Industrial Revolution*. London: Penguin.
15 Ritzer, G. (2004) *The McDonaldization of Society*. London: Sage.
16 Nurvala, J.P. (2015) '"Uberisation" Is the Future of the Digitalised Labour Market' *European View* 14, p. 231 https://doi.org/10.1007/s12290-015-0378-y
17 Monbiot, G. (2017) 'Forget "the Environment": We Need New Words to Convey Life's Wonders' *The Guardian* www.theguardian.com/commentisfree/2017/aug/09/forget-the-environment-new-words-lifes-wonders-language
18 Johnston, I. (2017) 'Global Mass Extinction Set to Begin by 2100, Study Finds' *The Independent* www.independent.co.uk/environment/mass-extinction-global-planet-start-year-2100-a7957886.html
19 Fettweis, G., and Zimmerman, E. (2017) 'ICT Energy Consumption: Trends and Challenges' *The 11th International Symposium on Wireless Personal Multimedia Communications* https://mns.ifn.et.tu-dresden.de/Lists/nPublications/Attachments/559/Fettweis_G_WPMC_08.pdf
20 Gammaitoni, L. (2016) 'Future ICT-Energy Concepts for Energy Efficiency & Sustainability' Workshop Summary Report *ICT-ENERGY.EU* https://ec.europa.eu/futurium/en/content/future-ict-energy-concepts-energy-efficiency-sustainability – Also see *ICT ENERGY LETTERS*, N. 12–1st August 2016 www.nanoenergyletters.com/files/nel/ICT-Energy_Letters_12.pdf?_ga=2.39450849.39594553.1508419207-1430191624.1508419207
21 See the infographic created by 911 Metallurgist available from www.911metallurgist.com
22 Gibson, W. (1993) *Neuromancer*. London: Harper Collins, p. 12.
23 Lanchester, J. (2017) 'You Are the Product' *London Review of Books* 39(16), pp. 3–10 www.lrb.co.uk/v39/n16/john-lanchester/you-are-the-product
24 Foer, F. (2017) 'Facebook's War on Free Will' *The Guardian* www.theguardian.com/technology/2017/sep/19/facebooks-war-on-free-will

25 Johnston, I. (2017) 'San Francisco Sues Big Oil for Billions over Climate Change Claiming They Knew the Dangers for Decades' *The Independent* www.independent.co.uk/environment/san-francisco-big-oil-lawsuit-climate-changes-fossil-fuels-knew-decades-tobacco-california-city-a7958871.html

26 Connell, R. (2007) *Southern Theory: The Global Dynamics of Knowledge in Social Science*. Cambridge: Polity Press.

27 Keynes, J.M. (1953) *The General Theory of Employment, Interest and Money*. New York: Harcourt Brace Jovanovich, p. 306. Quoted by Ghoshal, S. (2005) 'Bad Management Theories Are Destroying Good Management Practices' *Academy of Management Learning & Education* 4(1), pp. 75–91.

2 The problem with digital

This chapter begins with a brief overview of the research approaches in information systems as an academic field before turning to the deeper roots of its malaise in individualism and its looming consequences. The three branches of Information Systems research in academia prove to be a useful lens through which to understand the field: positivism, interpretivism, and the critical stance.

Positivism in information systems

To give it a very brief background summary, the 'scientism' at the root of positivism is not as old as the scientific approach itself. Descartes (1596–1650) was a devout Christian, the leading voice in the mainstream Enlightenment keen to 'defend the truth of revealed religion and the principle of the divinely created and ordered universe.'[1] But he made this defence whilst at the same time promoting the new 'mechanistic philosophy' enabling empirical scientific study of the 'natural' demarcated from the 'supernatural' by an exclusive focus upon the physically observable. When he thus spliced the universe in two, setting the world of thought and theology on one side as 'unknowables,' with the ordered and lawful world of mechanistic science on the other, the latter was uniquely susceptible to scientific experiment and – within a few decades, to Newton's Laws of Motion. This divide allowed the majority of lively minds to concentrate exclusively on science and leave theology – and the maintenance of monarchy, aristocracy, and theocracy – to the priests.[2] Thus, information derived from sensory experience, giving empirical findings, became deemed to be the exclusive source of evidential knowledge.[3] Comte (1798–1857) described this empirically 'derived' knowledge as 'positive' knowledge, giving birth to 'positivism.'[4] In time, all introspective or intuitive knowledge, and all metaphysics, came to be rejected as effectively theological.[5]

The fundamental problem with such positivism lies at its Cartesian root: if the mind – the space of the 'unknowables' – is placed beyond the physical, beyond space as such, then the two become so completely distinct in this divide that there is 'no conceptual model of their correlation and interaction'[6] – entirely contrary to common sense. We will look more closely at this in Chapters 3 and 4. For now, of most significance, is that Nature becomes defined by the scientific positivist approach which has evolved since Descartes, as something that does not include *us:* meaning not our bodies or brains, but the *persons* who observe and experience the sensations we label 'empirical.' Amongst philosophers there is both support for and rejection of this view that the only reality is an 'objective,' as opposed to 'subjective,' reality.

The positivism in positivist IS

Research in the Information Systems (IS) field is positivist: 'if there is evidence of formal propositions, quantifiable measures of variables, hypothesis testing, and the drawing of inferences about a phenomenon from a representative sample to a stated population.'[7] IS academic journals are prolifically populated with this kind of scholarship. It is clearly the main strength of positivist IS – that it clusters around formal processes and remains focussed upon practical concerns.

There are clear weaknesses, however, in this approach. As has been pointed out, some of this work, so strict in its formal processes, is not as practical as it professes, but, in fact, often quite 'irrelevant' to real problems in business contexts.[8] Mingers tells us that the problem with business schools attempting, since the 1960s, to attain academic rigour is that such work is 'rigorous in the sense of being highly quantitative and mathematical, but . . . far from the practical messy problems faced by real managers.'[9]

The high respectability of the physical sciences – the 'academic rigour' business schools in the 1960s began to wish to emulate – derives from the pre-war period of logical positivism, influenced by philosopher Bertrand Russell. The Vienna School of Logical Positivists, in the 1920s, professed a strict verificationism – the apotheosis of the positivist approach – which insisted that any proposition has no factual meaning if no evidence of observation can count for or against it. Thus, logical positivism is a doctrine where philosophy is relegated to being merely the handmaiden of science and all ethics, aesthetics, and romance deemed merely meaningless 'pseudo-statements.'[10] Economic historian Mirowski, in his *Machine Dreams*,[11] suggests that a story can be told of how throughout the middle of the 20th century the primacy of physics and mathematics can be linked to this very school of thought and the military-political usefulness of those engaged in it. Some pertinent elements of this story are worth including here, as they concern the history of business schools – the context in which IS grew up.[12]

David Hilbert's Göttingen School for gifted mathematicians, including his personal assistant, John von Neumann, in the late 1920s, was devoted to finding a complete and consistent set of axioms for all mathematics. But by 1931 Gödel had proven the inherent limitations of such logic – 'Any effectively generated theory capable of expressing elementary arithmetic cannot be both consistent and complete.'[13] This most famous of the 'incompleteness theorems' rendered Hilbert's mathematics programme a dead end. Moreover, Bertrand Russell's attempt to found philosophy in logic was thereby, arguably, equally doomed, for all the popularity of his *Principia Mathematica*, penned with Alfred North Whitehead. This, and Hitler's rise to power and purging of Jewish scholars from German universities in 1933, then brought Hilbert's school to a close. Von Neumann left Hilbert, Germany, and pure mathematics, and went into applied science, becoming an explosives expert in the employ of the US Defense Department. Here he contributed to Norbert Wiener's (one of Russell's students) cybernetics project in the RAD Lab at MIT – helping with the founding of cybernetics. He then helped Oppenheimer's Manhattan Project – the creation of the atom bomb. By the end of the war, moreover, von Neumann had penned the world's first comprehensive description of the design of an electronic stored-program computer, *First Draft of the Report on the EDVAC*, which 'rapidly became the design bible of the nascent computer community.'[14] Shortly thereafter, von Neumann sponsored Marschak and Koopman's computational and market-fundamentalist economics at the Cowles Foundation, which was soon to become the most powerful influence on the field of economics in the world.[15]

So, in the immensely influential person of John von Neumann, as with his fellow émigrés Carnap, Reichenbach, and Hempel, we can see Hilbert's project of axiomatising mathematics, and the logical positivism and verificationist attitude that went with it, were not altogether abandoned, but lowered to an applied science that still seemed to hold onto Hilbert's dream nonetheless and fed into cybernetics, the creation of the computer, and computational market-led economics. Von Neumann's background in mathematical logic, indeed, led him to believe fundamentally that both politics and economics were simply problems of logic. The notion of economic rationality, or 'rational man,' adopted by Marschak and Koopmans' Cowles Foundation and its thorough reconception of post-war economics, derived directly from von Neumann's influence. As Mirowski tells us, a 'profound sea change in the type of research being done at Cowles' took place, in which there was 'a noticeable turn . . . toward a reconceptualization of the "rational" economic agent as an information processor.'[16]

But as we have seen, the philosophy adhered to by this particular brand of economics (which still dominates business schools today), derived from von Neumann, among others, was a verificationist logical positivism that denied the existence of 'certain patently real phenomena'[17] such as the subjectivity of human existence. It may be tempting to think that businessmen, and their academic counterparts in business schools, are immune to the lofty musings of mathematicians, philosophers, economic theorists, and others. But not according to Keynes, as we saw in the introduction, who believed in the social power of ideas. Indeed, as Ghoshal reminded us, in 2005, 'Many of the worst excesses of recent management practices have their roots in a set of ideas that have emerged from business school academics over the last 30 years.'[18] There are numerous examples, but perhaps clearest is that corporate governance based upon Jensen and Meckling's agency theory, which[19] asserts that managers aren't to be trusted to do anything like managing. Maximising shareholder value is all that they should be doing, according to this theory, and therefore their interests and incentives, according to this theory, must be closely aligned with those of the shareholders by making stock options a significant part of their pay. 'Why then,' Ghoshal asks, 'do we feel surprised by the fact that executives in Enron, Global Crossing, Tyco, and scores of other companies granted themselves excessive stock options, treated their employees very badly, and took their customers for a ride when they could?'[20] Deeper still, however, as we shall see, is the pervasive methodological individualism of positivist thought, which treats all human beings as discrete individuals in a mathematical game whose 'rational' behaviour is to look after only their own interests, at the expense of others'.

In sum, the assumptions of 20th-century positivism are based upon a distinct logical positivist philosophy for whom the nature of Nature is exclusively 'objective,' and thus (i) discounts the human as part of its self-concept, and (ii) derives its sense of 'academic rigour' from the statistical methods of an economics that conceives of *Homo economicus* as an information processor. IS, in the eyes of the positivist, is (or at least should be) a physical science like physics or mathematics, harnessed for the making of profit.

Interpretivism

It is important to note that a good subset of those engaged in the Information Systems field are not positivists, and indeed many who still defer to positivist assumptions nonetheless also grant that those who do not nonetheless have an important contribution to make. 'Mixed methods' approaches, no less, are beginning to become the norm, too. So, what do Information Systems scholars do when they're not doing positivism? The interpretivist approach in IS evolved as early as the 1970s – Hirschheim and Klein's 'second era' of IS – but perhaps most substantively with the work of Peter

Checkland and the notion of 'soft systems.'[21] Nonetheless, little interpretive work was undertaken until the 1990s – Hirschheim and Klein's 'fourth era,' when IS began to move decisively beyond 'functionalist philosophical assumptions.'[22] Through the International Federation for Information Processing (IFIP)'s Technical Committee 8 (TC8) on Information Systems, and Technical Committee 9 (TC9) on ICT and Society, and increasingly in the IS journals,[23] interpretivism homed in on the social aspects of information systems, and this is clearly the great strength of this approach. Interpretive IS research is concerned with 'human thought and action in social and organizational contexts,' according to Klein and Myers,[24] and if IS is considered a spectrum between computing and sociology, then interpretivism is certainly anchored toward the latter end.

The positivism in interpretive IS

This strength can also, however, if the more practical concerns are not given proper weight, at the same time, be a weakness. Though there have been some very interesting critiques of the position that our knowledge of reality is gained *only* through social constructions, and serious attempts to move on from it[25,26,27] noted by some IS scholars,[28,29] some interpretive IS research has focused upon the human almost to the exclusion of the IT artefacts themselves.[30,31] Interpretivism arguably promotes a worldview in which events can never be objectively observed from the outside, but can only be observed from inside through the direct experience of people involved in those events – even when the direct experience is that of the researcher, observing the events from outside: the reflexivity of the observer is indeed often a (laudable) feature of such research. The split between subject and object, achieved by positivism, is thereby in fact maintained, in some interpretive work, and no resolution achieved.

As Klein and Myers point out, a fundamental principle in interpretivism concerns the hermeneutic circle, which 'suggests that we come to understand a complex whole from preconceptions about the meanings of its parts and their interrelationships.'[32] Here, perhaps, interpretivists might take pause. There are preconceptions – philosophical groundings, or 'fore-projections' in hermeneutical terminology[33] – about the nature of Nature, derived from positivism, which many interpretivists in fact, albeit unwittingly, continue and support when they perpetuate the divide between the objective and the subjective. The principle of contextualisation is key here, for as Klein and Myers point out, it '[r]equires critical reflection of the social and historical background of the research setting, so that the intended audience can see how the current situation under investigation emerged.'[34] A proper contextualisation, then, should include the background of views on the nature of Nature by which a whole range of decisions based on 'objective' phenomena to the exclusion of 'subjective' phenomena (or vice versa) have predetermined both the context and its modes of interpretation. The hermeneutic circle, in other words, sometimes carries 'fore-projections' just as positivist as the positivists, when it is assumed 'our knowledge of reality is gained *only* through social constructions.' Karakayali[35] rightly points out the ontological dilemma in a great deal of sociology between those who 'demarcate social reality as a causally autonomous and qualitatively distinct realm,' on the one hand, and those, on the other, including Actor Network Theory (ANT) theorists and the New Materialists such as Barad, van der Tuin, Winner, and others, who have 'postulated a more open (or flat) ontological space and blurred such demarcations.'[36] This book – as we shall see in Chapter 3 – addresses directly and fundamentally the fiction of such demarcations, wherever they may be found.

The critical stance

In many respects 'the conservatism of the IS discipline'[37] belongs most obviously in its positivist wing. However, although often 'interpretivist methods have been used to gather material for critical analyses,'[38] most interpretivist IS research fights shy of critique, preferring to leave such conclusions to the reader: one might say that many interpretivists can be in some ways as conservative as the positivists. But what of those scholars engaged in critical IS? As Kathy McGrath describes, interpretive researchers commonly seek 'multiple interpretations and deep understanding of the often conflicting rationalities of the people' engaged in IS innovation. Critical researchers, by contrast, 'often have a cause – for example, feminism, environmentalism, less developed economies.'[39] This would suggest, perhaps, that at least some critical IS scholars are interpretivists with a particular 'beef,' who wish to make a political point through their scholarship in support of their particular passion. This is perhaps the greatest strength of critical IS – that significant agendas can be foregrounded and pursued through it.

More broadly, critical IS research, as Myers and Klein put it, 'can be classified as critical if the main task is seen as being one of social critique, whereby the restrictive and alienating conditions of the status quo are brought to light.'[40] Orlikowski and Baroudi,[41] Walsham,[42] Lyytinen,[43] and Avgerou[44] have all identified particular critical theories and concepts as promising ones for the discipline and have argued that 'although there are no critical methods as such, interpretive methods can help in the field.'[45] Now critical IS has a long pedigree, with its nascent stirrings as early as those of interpretivism. As McGrath points out, the proceedings of the first *Human Choice and Computers* conference in 1974 include an encouragement by editors Mumford and Sackman 'to engage with the way that computer applications were being developed and deployed, and to make the human choices necessary to ensure that democratic values and ideals were preserved for the benefit of everyone.'[46] IFIP's TC9 – convened in 1976 in response to this very conference, which it then made its own – has continued to pursue this course.[47]

In the 1980s critical IS began to flower, with the use of Habermas by Lyytinen and Klein,[48] and the arrival of sociologists in British business schools bringing with them the ideas of Foucault and Bourdieu,[49,50] and by the 1990s was gaining increasing acceptance in the field.[51] The aim, as Helen Richardson and Brian Robinson put it, was to undertake a 'critique of the illusions and contradictions of social existence with a view to enabling and encouraging social change.'[52] A weakness of critical IS, then, may be that it is focussed upon the concerns of those who in the 1980s arrived in business schools and brought their favoured critical thinkers with them. Are these, in other words, the right or best concerns that critical IS should be addressing?

Conservatism in critical IS

My question is whether a certain 'conservatism in IS' is affecting critical IS too. Although other critical approaches have been put forward[53,54] the streams identified by Myers and Klein[55] around Habermas, Foucault, and Bourdieu seem to be creating strong clusters of scholars speaking to one another. Whether this can develop into a 'political movement,' as Grey[56] suggests, 'challenging the direction of IS both as an academic discipline and as applied outside the academy' remains to be seen. I agree that critical IS needs to become more relevant outside of its own internal discussions, but am unclear how the streams identified by Myers and Klein are likely to achieve this.

Perhaps critical IS, in search of insight, can and should go deeper than Habermas, Foucault, or Bourdieu. All three might be characterised as working in the area of epistemology – that branch of philosophy concerned with the theory of knowledge. Ontology, on the other hand, is a branch of philosophy concerned with the nature of existence itself and, until logical positivism arrived claiming to discount it entirely, was a branch of the wider field of metaphysics, the ultimate philosophical enquiry into what *is* and what it is like. Russell's dismissal of metaphysics as little more than theology seems like a sleight of hand, throwing a veil over questions he, and fellow positivists, perhaps didn't want people to ask or to seek answers to. Critical IS research, I believe, should delve into metaphysics, specifically the underpinnings of philosophies of science and concepts of Nature, as I will do in the next chapter, to challenge the assumptions upon which positivism is based and challenge the status quo that some interpretivism merely observes. This, I believe, is the depth to which critical IS should go.

Information systems as an academic field: a summary

In sum, we can say that the field of Information Systems is not only rooted in 1920s logical positivism, since its birth in post-war business schools that were wedded to an economic orthodoxy founded in that philosophy, but that a natural conservatism in the field keeps it anchored to those roots. The interpretivist and critical wings of the field, moreover, seem quite clipped by the parental positivist core of the discipline – at least ontologically. The digital world this field has spawned, meanwhile, from the sapling of mainframe-linked business terminals in post-war office blocks, has become a giant tree of social software, always-on communication, and immersive digital experience. In this urban bath of wireless signals, each of us is rendered – counter-intuitively – as an isolated and discrete individual by the very information communication technologies that seem to connect us. As Sherry Turkle memorably depicts the reality of the smartphone world, we are 'Alone Together,'[57] our every contact with one another mediated by the technologies that keep us apart as they connect us, compromising our well-being.[58] This is happening because the philosophy of logical positivism dismisses all the emotional intelligence of human body language, ignores the fundamental interrelatedness and contingency of our identities, and reduces our behaviour to game-theory bottom lines of self-interest that are then programmed into the devices and platforms that purport to connect us.

Individualism

Methodological individualism

The computational market-fundamentalist form of economics sponsored by the Cowles men in the 1950s centred around notions of the individual rational actor as an information processor. Yet as Bernd Stahl[59] points out, such a 'methodological individualism' – assumed in much positivist IS literature – is a philosophical choice, and one that should be questioned. Methodological individualism, as defined by Lukes, 'is a doctrine about explanation which asserts that all attempts to explain social (or individual) phenomena are to be rejected . . . unless they are couched wholly in terms of facts about individuals.'[60] As Lukes elucidates, definitions of individuals must be very narrow, restricted only to descriptions of the most material type (I – genetic make-up, brain states, etc.) or of the most personal type (II – aggression, gratification, etc.), if individuals are to be understood in the absence of any wider considerations. The moment any minimal social references enter descriptions of individuals (type III – cooperation, power, esteem, etc.), then functional, collective, or social explanations begin to have meaning, and with descriptions that are maximally social (type IV – cashing cheques, saluting, voting), propositions about groups and institutions are presupposed, or even directly entailed. But the assumptions of market-fundamentalist economics – of the rational actor as information processor – are built upon a methodological individualism that discounts all functional, collective social entities or action in favour of individuals defined only in terms of types I and II: what Macpherson describes as the assumptions of 'possessive individualism [in] . . . a possessive market society.'[61] Methodological individualism, in the economic orthodoxy of business schools, runs through the core of business information systems and is as apparent today in the 'social' platforms of digital culture: we are, indeed, 'Alone Together.'[62]

Very broadly speaking, though with notable exceptions and attempts at resolution, Anglo-American thinkers (Hobbes, Locke, Hayek, Popper, Nozick) have preferred methodological individualism and focussed more upon the first two types of descriptions of individuals (I – genetic make-up, brain states, etc.; II – aggression, gratification, etc.), and Continental ones (Comte, Durkheim, Hegel, Marx, Cohen) have preferred functional explanations and focussed more upon the latter two (type III – cooperation, power, esteem, etc.; type IV – cashing cheques, saluting, voting).

Possessive individualism

The Anglo-American form of individualism, moreover, is at its root, as MacPherson described it, a 'possessive individualism.' This 'possessive individualism,' where methodological individualism is harnessed for self-interest, begins with the ownership of the self and moves rapidly into the appropriation of the 'unowned' – a term central to the ideas of British philosopher John Locke. For Locke, writing in the 17th century, that which is unowned can become owned when mixed with the labour of a self-owning individual: in this sense, he is a founding (philosophical) father of the United States. He was also a slave owner with shares in the trade.[63] However, Locke qualifies this with a proviso: that there is enough and as good left in common for others. 'No body could think himself injured by the drinking of another man,' he says, 'though he took a good draught, who had a whole river of the same water left him to quench his thirst: and the case of land and water, where there is enough of both, is perfectly the same.'[64] In the colonial expansion, if one can set the ethnic cleansing of Native Americans[65] aside, then the appropriation of land by British colonists in the Americas is 'just' if they till the land with their own labour (or that of the slaves they own). The land is 'unowned' because the natives have no 'title' to it, and there is, of course, plenty of land for all – once the natives have been 'exterminated' as Jefferson later put it[66] – so long as the new continent is not 'claimed' by a monarch (much more important to Locke) who is, after all, not tilling the land with his own hand. Locke's notions of ownership, therefore, of both self and property, boil down ultimately to the reasoning behind the creation of settler colonies by British entrepreneurs (i) without monarchical interference, (ii) with the use of slave labour imported from Africa, and (iii) once the indigenous natives had been cleared out of the way. The archetypal 'individual,' then – derived from Locke – is a capitalist entrepreneur defined by his independence from monarchical control, ownership of slave labour, and disregard for indigenous people in the way of his land grab. As Jane Mansbridge described it, Locke lived in a society where 'self-interest [was] advanced as a weapon against a monarch who used the language of public interest to promote foreign adventure.'[67] For Locke, such foreign adventure should be private, not public.

In the late 20th century, as part of the ongoing apology for this 17th-century behaviour, US philosopher Robert Nozick, a man at the philosophical heart of neoliberal political philosophy, takes this notion of the appropriation of the unowned and says it is 'just,' with the proviso that others are not thereby made worse off. We will take Nozick to task in Chapter 4. Meanwhile, it is clear, as Macpherson puts it, that the 'possessive quality' of the individualism put forward by Locke – and remodelled by Nozick – not only conceives of the individual as the proprietor of his or her own person and capacities, *but that she or he owes nothing to society for them*. In practice, then, Locke's proviso granted rights and freedoms to English capitalists to displace Native Americans and appropriate tracts of land in the New World, to be worked by African slaves. In practice, too, Nozick's proviso grants American capitalists rights and freedoms to monopolise the means of production, so long as wages are paid that make others better off than if they had no wages at all.

Inert nature

Methodological individualism and a positivist stance also applied to our understanding of our environment for much of the founding decades of the science of ecology. There is not space for an in-depth treatment here, and a few examples will need to suffice. I refer the reader to my book, *Bergson, Complexity and Creative Emergence*, for further detail. The three examples here concern (i) the influences upon Darwin, (ii) the development of the notion of ecosystems, and (iii) the post-war science of ecology.

Darwin

Let us start with Darwin's 1859 classic *The Origin of Species*.[68] Prior to his voyage upon HMS *Beagle*, Darwin had read and been influenced by astronomer Herschel's book, *A Preliminary Discourse on the Study of Natural Philosophy*. For Herschel nature was governed by laws which it should be the highest aim of natural philosophy to discern.[69] A powerful influence over all academic and practical pursuits in the 19th century was the idea that all things could be worked out mathematically; that the neat equations of Newton and Hamilton could find their equivalents in all fields of scientific endeavour; and that the point of science was to describe life, the universe, and everything in such terms. For all the famed innovation of his work, Darwin was a scientist of his time, keen to fit well within this scientific consensus. One example of this will suffice.

Darwin's greatest 'borrowing' from the ideas of his time was the notions of competition and struggle in the economic and social theory of Scottish Enlightenment figure, Adam Smith.[70] As the great evolutionary biologist Stephen Jay Gould describes it, 'Darwin transferred the paradoxical argument of Adam Smith's economics into biology (best organisation for the general polity arising as a side consequence of permitting individuals to struggle for themselves alone) in order to devise a mechanism – natural selection.'[71] It is clear from Darwin's own notebooks that he read Adam Smith, and not just the famous *Wealth of Nations*, but his *Essays on Philosophical Subjects* too,[72] and although Darwin does not mention Smith in *The Origin of Species* he does so in his later work, *The Descent of Man*.[73]

Schweber tells us, 'It is his study of Dugald Stewart and particularly of Adam Smith which reinforced [Darwin's] focus on the individual as the central element and unit in his theory and led him to adopt the Scottish view of trying to understand the whole in terms of the individual parts and their interactions'[74] – the classic methodological individualist approach. Darwin spent much of the late 1830s trying to find a 'quantitative, mathematical'[75] formulation that was 'deterministic.'[76] Natural selection, moreover, Schweber informs us, was an idea Darwin had originally gleaned from pamphlets by Sebright and Wilkingson on animal breeding: 'As perceived by Sebright, artificial selection acts analogously to "Nature's broom" by eliminating inferior variations.'[77] It was, moreover, from 'the writings of Adam Smith and the other Scottish Common Sense philosophers that Darwin initially got his emphasis on individuals as the units for his theory of natural selection,'[78] contrary to his earlier focus upon species as the units of selection,[79] and, as Gould tells us, contrary indeed to his final acceptance that species must be considered units of selection as well as individuals.[80]

From these 'origins' then, one could conclude that stock breeding, a socio-academic requirement for a quantitative and deterministic theory, and the rather paradoxical, reductionist Smithian economics that heap all macro events onto the behaviour of individuals, all came together in Darwin's mind to cause his focus upon 'natural selection' as the sole mechanism of evolution. Contemporary evolutionary theory, as Gould stated in 2002, 'must be construed as basically different from the canonical theory of natural selection, rather than simply extended.'[81]

Ecosystems and social Darwinism

Decades later, when Tansley coined the term 'ecosystems' in a 1935 paper in the journal, *Ecology*, of which he was the editor, it was in fact by way of criticising his ecological colleague Clements' holism.[82] Polymath Herbert Spencer had produced an influential paper, *The Social Organism*,[83] a year after Darwin's classic, in 1860. Spencer was one of the most powerful voices in 19th-century academia, a proponent of the notion of evolution even before Darwin, and a classical liberal political theorist. It is from Spencer that the oft-quoted phrase 'survival of the fittest' stems.[84] But this 'social Darwinism' not only stressed individualism, but developed into an apology for white supremacy and European colonialism. Smuts' 1926 book *Holism and Evolution*[85] (the basic holistic premise of which was adopted by Clements)[86] made no pretence to scientific validity, happily suggesting that due to the immeasurable length of geological time no laboratory-based experiments could prove or disprove his thesis.[87] Nonetheless, Smuts believed, the principle of wholes gathered together in ever greater wholes, up to and including the ultimate totality, was a sufficient principle for the understanding of life and of society. This thesis, written in opposition between periods as prime minister of South Africa, was no doubt suited to a politician (and general) of the British Empire and vigorous proponent of the League of Nations. It was also, unfortunately, well suited to an equally vigorous proponent, as he was, of segregation between what he regarded as the evolutionarily advanced white race and the black races of the continent over much of which his empire ruled. These segregation rules formed the foundation of the later apartheid. Smuts' holism was the target, and a mathematical notion of 'ecosystems' the weapon, for Tansley, in his tussle with Clements for the helm of the new science of ecology. By the time Bertalanffy[88] began to use the notion of systems for a broader 'systems thinking' much of the later information systems community would engage in, both the social Darwinist and the mathematicised ecosystemic approach, were in play in the background of scholarly assumptions.

Ecosystems and irradiated atolls

A final example takes place in the 1940s. Famous early 20th-century ecologist Hutchinson took Walter B. Cannon's notion of feedback as a basis with which to model the behaviour of populations in the wild. Hutchinson[89] and others (in particular Lindeman)[90] brought the tenets of cybernetics into ecology and proceeded to further mathematicise it. Hutchinson and Lindeman developed a quasi-algebraic language to represent and calculate the behaviour of species and their populations, built on the cybernetic principles of self-regulation and feedback tending back toward equilibrium and rest.

This move successfully recast the notion of ecosystems in axiomatic, logical, and mechanical terms. It will be no surprise that John von Neumann was a key influence upon both Hutchinson and Lindemann. Much ecosystems research was undertaken in the 1950s – largely by the Odum brothers – on irradiated atolls in the Pacific, following nuclear tests. A transformation of ecological metaphors – 'a gradual shift from organic to machine images'[91] – took place as the 1950s unfolded. Coral reefs became 'self-regulating systems' in this new language of ecology, represented by Hutchinson and Lindeman's algebraic formulae, to the point where Howard Odum could declare, in 1959, that '[t]he relationships between producer plants and consumer animals, between predator and prey, not to mention the numbers and kinds of organisms in a given environment, are all limited and controlled by the same basic laws which govern non-living systems, such as electric motors and automobiles.'[92]

Life, by the efforts of cybernetics-inspired ecologists, then, was reduced, throughout much of the 20th century as the science of ecology arose, to mathematical formulae describing the observed behaviour of individuals: methodological individualism once more. In the 1960s cybernetics textbooks were taught in ecology classes in universities.[93] Second-order cybernetics, from the 1960s onwards, began to reintroduce the observer into such systems, and finally complexity theory unpicked the neat loops to expose the radical contingency and sheer complexity such simple pictures had hidden. It took a revolution in ideas in the 1990s for ecology finally to change, as we will see in Chapter 4.

In short, the logical positivism and methodological individualism of John von Neumann's computational science not only discounted all subjective aspects of our humanity in its depiction of us as rational economic actors pursuing self-interest, it rendered the living natural world around us into a collection of discrete, inert individuals subject to the same economic rules of struggle and the mathematical formulae of competitive advantage. There are, however, very different ways of looking at the world, as we shall explore in the next chapter.

Notes

1 Israel, J. (2002) *Radical Enlightenment: Philosophy and the Making of Modernity 1650–1750*. Oxford: Oxford University Press, p. 15.
2 ibid., p. 19.

3 Klein, H.K., and Lyytinen, K. (1985) 'The Poverty of Scientism in Information Systems' in *Research Methods in Information Systems*, Mumford, E. et al. (eds.). Amsterdam: Elsevier Science.
4 Comte, A., and Bridges, J.H. (tr.) (1865/2009) *A General View of Positivism*. Trubner and Co., reissued by Cambridge: Cambridge University Press.
5 Russell, B. (1914) *The Philosophy of Bergson*. Cambridge: Bowes and Bowes.
6 Capek, M. (1987) 'Bergson's Theory of the Mind-Brain Relation' in *Bergson and Modern Thought*, Papanicolaou, A. and Gunter, P. (eds.), p. 132. Chur: Harwood Academic Publishers.
7 Klein, H.K., and Myers, M.D. (1999) 'A Set of Principles for Conducting and Evaluating Interpretive Field Studies in Information Systems' *MIS Quarterly* 23(1), p. 69.
8 Checkland, P. (1980) 'The Systems Movement and the "Failure" of Management Science' *Cybernetics and Systems* 11, pp. 317–324.
9 Mingers, J. (2015) 'Helping Business Schools Engage with Real Problems: The Contribution of Critical Realism and Systems Thinking' *European Journal of Operational Research* 242, pp. 316–331.
10 Carnap, R. (1932) 'The Elimination of Metaphysics through Logical Analysis of Language' *Erkenntnis*, pp. 60–81.
11 Mirowski, P. (2002) *Machine Dreams: Economics Becomes a Cyborg Science*. Cambridge: Cambridge University Press.
12 Hirschheim, R., and Klein, H. (2012) 'A Glorious and Not-So-Short History of the Information Systems Field' *Journal of the Association for Information Systems* 13(4), p. 193.
13 Kleene, S. (1967/2001) *Mathematical Logic*. New York: John Wiley, p. 250.
14 Mirowski, P. (2002) *Machine Dreams: Economics Becomes a Cyborg Science*. Cambridge: Cambridge University Press, p. 176.
15 ibid., p. 157.
16 ibid., p. 215.
17 Nagel, T. (1986) *The View from Nowhere*. Oxford: Oxford University Press, p. 7.
18 Ghoshal, S. (2005) 'Bad Management Theories Are Destroying Good Management Practices' *Academy of Management Learning & Education* 4(1), p. 75.
19 Jensen, M., and Meckling, W. (1976) 'Theory of the Firm: Managerial Behaviour, Agency Costs and Ownership Structure' *Journal of Financial Economics* 3, pp. 305–360.
20 Ghoshal, S. (2005) 'Bad Management Theories Are Destroying Good Management Practices' *Academy of Management Learning & Education* 4(1), p. 76.
21 Checkland, P. (1980) 'The Systems Movement and the "Failure" of Management Science' *Cybernetics and Systems* 11, pp. 317–324.
22 Hirschheim, R., and Klein, H. (2012) 'A Glorious and Not-So-Short History of the Information Systems Field' *Journal of the Association for Information Systems* 13(4), pp. 216–217.
23 ibid., p. 217.
24 Klein, H.K., and Myers, M.D. (1999) 'A Set of Principles for Conducting and Evaluating Interpretive Field Studies in Information Systems' *MIS Quarterly* 23(1), p. 67.
25 Hacking, I. (1999) *The Social Construction of What?* London: Harvard University Press.
26 Schatzki, T., Cetina, K., and Savignu, E. (eds.) (2001) *The Practice Turn in Contemporary Theory*. Abingdon, Oxon, UK: Routledge.
27 Barad, K. (2007) *Meeting the Universe Halfway*. London: Duke University Press.

28 e.g. Orlikowski, W. (2005) 'Material Works: Exploring the Situated Entanglement of Technological Performativity and Human Agency' *Scandinavian Journal of Information Systems* 17(1), pp. 183–186.
29 Mingers, J. (2015) 'Helping Business Schools Engage with Real Problems: The Contribution of Critical Realism and Systems Thinking' *European Journal of Operational Research* 242.
30 Orlikowski, W., and Iacono, S. (2001) 'Research Commentary: Desperately Seeking the "IT" in IT Research: A Call to Theorizing the IT Artifact' *Information Systems Research* 12(2), pp. 121–134.
31 Benbasat, I., and Zmud, R.W. (2003) 'The Identity Crisis within the IS Discipline: Defining and Communicating the Discipline's Core Properties' *MIS Quarterly*, pp. 183–194.
32 Klein, H.K., and Myers, M.D. (1999) 'A Set of Principles for Conducting and Evaluating Interpretive Field Studies in Information Systems' *MIS Quarterly* 23(1), p. 71.
33 Hassan, N.R. (2014) 'Paradigm Lost . . . Paradigm Gained: A Hermeneutical Rejoinder to Banville and Landry's "Can the Field of MIS Be Disciplined?" ' *European Journal of Information Systems* 23(6), pp. 600–615.
34 Klein, H.K., and Myers, M.D. (1999) 'A Set of Principles for Conducting and Evaluating Interpretive Field Studies in Information Systems' *MIS Quarterly* 23(1), p. 72.
35 Karakayali, N. (2015) 'Two Ontological Orientations in Sociology: Building Social Ontologies and Blurring the Boundaries of the "Social"' *Sociology* 49(4), pp. 732–747.
36 ibid., p. 732.
37 Walsham, G. (2005a) 'Learning about Being Critical' *Information Systems Journal* 15, pp. 111–117.
38 Richardson, H., and Robinson, B. (2007) 'The Mysterious Case of the Missing Paradigm: A Review of Critical Information Systems Research' *Information Systems Journal* 17(3), p. 260.
39 McGrath, K. (2005) 'Doing Critical Research in Information Systems: A Case of Theory and Practice Not Informing Each Other' *Information Systems Journal* 15, p. 86.
40 Klein, H.K., and Myers, M.D. (1999) 'A Set of Principles for Conducting and Evaluating Interpretive Field Studies in Information Systems' *MIS Quarterly* 23(1), p. 69.
41 Orlikowski, W., and Baroudi, J. (1991) 'Studying Information Technology in Organizations: Research Approaches and Assumptions' *Information Systems Research* 2, pp. 1–28.
42 Walsham, G. (2003) 'Development, Global Futures and IS Research: A Polemic' *Closing Keynote Address to the IFIP WG 8.2 and IFIP WG 9.4 Conference*. Athens University of Economics and Business, Greece.
43 Lyytinen, K. (1992) 'Information Systems and Critical Theory' in *Critical Management Studies*, Alvesson, M. and Willmott, H. (eds.), pp. 159–180. London, UK: Sage.
44 Avgerou, C. (2002) *Information Systems and Global Diversity*. Oxford, UK: Oxford University Press.
45 McGrath, K. (2005) 'Doing Critical Research in Information Systems: A Case of Theory and Practice Not Informing Each Other' *Information Systems Journal* 15, p. 86.
46 ibid., p. 87.

47 Kreps, D., Fletcher, G., and Griffiths, M. (2016) 'Human Choice and Computers: An Ever More Intimate Relationship' in *Technology and Intimacy: Choice or Coercion 12th IFIP TC 9 International Conference on Human Choice and Computers, HCC12 2016, Salford, UK, September 7–9, 2016, Proceedings*, Kreps, D., Fletcher, G., and Griffiths, M. (eds.). London, UK: Springer.
48 Lyytinen, K., and Klein, H.K. (1985) 'The Critical Theory of Jurgen Habermas as a Basis for a Theory of Information Systems' in *Research Methods in Information Systems*, Mumford, E., Hirschheim, R.A., Fitzgerald, G., and Wood-Harper, A.T. (eds.), pp. 207–226. Amsterdam: North-Holland.
49 Carter, C. (2008) 'A Curiously British Story: Foucault Goes to Business School' *International Studies of Management and Organisation* 38(1), pp. 13–29.
50 Myers, M.D., and Klein, H.K. (2011) 'A Set of Principles for Conducting Critical Research in Information Systems' *MIS Quarterly* 35(1), p. 19.
51 Hirschheim, R., and Klein, H. (2012) 'A Glorious and Not-So-Short History of the Information Systems Field' *Journal of the Association for Information Systems* 13(4), pp. 216–217.
52 Richardson, H., and Robinson, B. (2007) 'The Mysterious Case of the Missing Paradigm: A Review of Critical Information Systems Research' *Information Systems Journal* 17(3), p. 254.
53 Fournier, V., and Grey, C. (2000) 'At the Critical Moment: Conditions and Prospects for Critical Management Studies' *Human Relations* 53(1), pp. 7–32.
54 Howcroft, D., and Trauth, E. (2005) *Handbook of Critical Information Systems Research: Theory and Application*. Cheltenham: Edward Elgar.
55 Myers, M.D., and Klein, H.K. (2011) 'A Set of Principles for Conducting Critical Research in Information Systems' *MIS Quarterly* 35(1), pp. 17–36.
56 Grey, C. (2005) 'Critical Management Studies: Towards a More Mature Politics' in *Handbook of Critical Information Systems Research: Theory and Application*, Howcroft, D. and Trauth, E. (eds.), pp. 174–194. Cheltenham, UK: Edward Elgar.
57 Turkle, S. (2011) *Alone Together*. Philadelphia, PA: Basic Books.
58 Shakya, H.B., and Christakis, N.A. (2017) 'Association of Facebook Use with Compromised Well-Being: A Longitudinal Study' *American Journal of Epidemiology* 1; 185(3), pp. 203–211 doi: 10.1093/aje/kww189
59 Stahl, B. (2008) *Information Systems: Critical Perspectives*. London: Routledge, p. 135.
60 Lukes, S. (1973) *Individualism*. Oxford: Blackwell, p. 12.
61 MacPherson, C.B. (1962/2011) *The Political Theory of Possessive Individualism: Hobbes to Locke*. Oxford: Clarendon Press, p. 271.
62 Turkle, S. (2011) *Alone Together*. Philadelphia, PA: Basic Books.
63 Farr, J. (2007) 'So Vile and Miserable an Estate: The Problem of Slavery in Locke's Political Thought' *Political Theory* 14(2), pp. 263–289.
64 Locke, J. (1689) Second Treatise of Government www.gutenberg.org/ebooks/7370V:33
65 Mann, M. (2006) *The Dark Side of Democracy: Explaining Ethnic Cleansing*. Cambridge: Cambridge University Press.
66 ibid., p. ix.
67 Mansbridge, J. (1990) *Beyond Self-Interest*. Chicago: University of Chicago Press, p. 5.
68 Darwin, C. (1859) On the Origin of Species: An Electronic Classics Series Publication www2.hn.psu.edu/faculty/jmanis/darwin/originspecies.pdf

69 Darwin, C. (1887) The Autobiography of Charles Darwin, Darwin Online http://darwin-online.org.uk/content/frameset?viewtype=text&itemID=F1497&pageseq=69
70 Smith, A. (1776/1977) *An Inquiry into the Nature and Causes of the Wealth of Nations*. Chicago: University of Chicago Press.
71 Gould, S.J. (2002) *The Structure of Evolutionary Theory*. Cambridge, MA: Harvard University Press, p. 59.
72 Darwin, C.R. *Notebook M: [Metaphysics on Morals and Speculations on Expression (1838)]*. CUL-DAR125. Transcribed by K. Rookmaaker, edited by P. Barrett. (*Darwin Online* http://darwin-online.org.uk/), p. 109.
73 Darwin, C.R. (1871) *The Descent of Man, and Selection in Relation to Sex*. London: John Murray, Volume 1, p. 81
74 Schweber, S.S. (1977) 'The Origin of the *Origin* Revisited' *Journal of the History of Biology* 10(2), p. 233.
75 ibid., p. 232.
76 ibid.
77 ibid.
78 ibid., p. 277.
79 ibid., p. 278.
80 Gould, S.J. (2002) *The Structure of Evolutionary Theory*. Cambridge, MA: Harvard University Press, p. 36.
81 ibid., p. 3.
82 Tansley, A. (1935) 'The Use and Abuse of Vegetational Concepts and Terms' *Ecology* 16(3), pp. 284–307.
83 Spencer, H. (1860) *The Social Organism* First Published in *The Westminster Review* for January 1860 and Reprinted in *Spencer's Essays: Scientific, Political and Speculative*. London and New York, 1892, in three volumes www.econlib.org/library/LFBooks/Spencer/spnMvS9.html
84 Spencer, H. (1964) *Principles of Biology*. Williams and Norgate, p. 444 https://archive.org/stream/principlesbiolo05spengoog#page/n10/mode/2up
85 Smuts, J. (1926) Holism and Evolution https://archive.org/details/holismevolution00smut
86 See Hagen, J.B. (1992) *An Entangled Bank*. New Brunswick, NJ: Rutgers University Press, pp. 84–85.
87 Smuts, J. (1926) *Holism and Evolution*, p. 226 https://archive.org/details/holismevolution00smut
88 Bertalanffy, L. (1950) 'Theory of Open Systems in Physics and Biology' *Science* 111(2872), pp. 23–29.
89 Hagen, J.B. (1992) *An Entangled Bank*. New Brunswick, NJ: Rutgers University Press, pp. 64–68.
90 ibid., pp. 87–97.
91 ibid., p. 126.
92 Odum, H. (1959) *Fundamentals of Ecology* (2nd ed.). Philadelphia: Saunders & Co., p. 44.
93 Hagen, J.B. (1992) *An Entangled Bank*. New Brunswick, NJ: Rutgers University Press, p. 132.

3 The future does not exist

It would take many books, and not just one chapter, to do justice to the full breadth and depth of process philosophy. I can here only provide a selective introduction, and that selection, as I pointed out earlier, is inevitably subjective. Nonetheless, as will become clear, the subjective is not to be dismissed as lacking rigour and foundation, rationality or depth, and it is indeed a clear focus of much work in process philosophy. In his very accessible introduction to Alfred North Whitehead's *Process-Relational Philosophy*, C. Robert Mesle has summed up beautifully – to my mind – the fundamental distinction between the broad sweep of Western philosophy and the essence of process philosophy. Mesle relates a sudden, gestalt realisation that came to him in an 'Of course!'[1] moment standing by Lake Michigan, staring across the waves: *the future does not exist*. One imagines a similar moment taking place, between 1881 and 1883, for Henri Bergson, who 'saw, to my great astonishment,' as he told American philosopher William James in a letter of 1908, 'that scientific time does not *endure*, that it would involve no change in our scientific knowledge if the totality of the real were unfolded all at once, instantaneously.'[2] Bergson saw that *the future does not exist*.

For Bergson the 'time' of science is simply a collection of 'instants' laid out side by side in space, and not in fact anything that endures at all. Yet real time, the *durée reélle* as he calls it, is something that each and every one of us knows immediately, because we live it. The time of positive science, for Bergson, determines all existence from beginning to end in a fixed, mechanical grip. Yet lived time, for all that the possible is constrained, is bounded at the crest of the now by many potential futures, and it is often conscious choice which decides which way things will unfold. Whitehead, acknowledging his debt to Bergson,[3] saw this too. 'Decisions must be made; the future must be created. The creatures of the present must decide between many possibilities for what may happen, and their collective decisions bring the new moment into being.'[4]

The difference between these two understandings of the nature of time reveals a fundamental truth about the nature of reality. For all the seeming permanence of abstract notions such as 2 + 2 = 4 – surely an eternal truism that will never change – they remain abstract notions. Reality, however, is by nature impermanent, and change is the only constant. That most famous of ancient Greek philosophers, Plato, focussed upon the abstract as the most important – because the most permanent – giving birth to the Theory of Forms – the reification of the world of Ideas over the messy and imprecise world of ever-changing reality. This Platonic universe, in which the permanent and immaterial was valued over the impermanent stuff of the real, has, in certain respects, remained ascendant in Western philosophy ever since. It has been frequently challenged, beginning with those amongst Plato's contemporaries – including Epicurus – who encouraged us to focus, instead, upon the actuality of the real. It has also been cleverly amended, shifting the comforting permanence of the abstract down to a new understanding of the real as a collection of fixed and permanent 'things.'

Philosophers have struggled for centuries over how best to characterise 'the relationship between Being and Becoming.'[5] In the West, since Plato, we have focussed largely upon Being. The God of the Christians is permanent, abstract, omnipotent, omniscient, creates and stands outside of time, and watches its unfolding as if playing a recording. 'From God's perspective, which surely defines ultimate reality, nothing new happens, nothing changes.'[6]

At the dawn of the modern era, René Descartes and, not long after, Isaac Newton, also 'argued for Being over Becoming by insisting . . . that the world is composed of physical and mental "substances."'[7] The key feature of these new fixed 'things' – whether physical or mental – in the real world, for Descartes and Newton, was that they are measurable, susceptible to precise determinations by experiments which can tell us exact and definite details about the 'things' in question. Thus, the Christian world of permanence was very neatly imported into the new world of material science, and the two progressed happily together from there for several hundred years. As Bruno Latour[8] pointed out, however, the conditions of laboratory science are as abstract as the knowledge they give to us: that knowledge, indeed, is about how things are within the precise – and static – conditions of laboratory science; 'things' in the real world are not quite the same.

Most significantly, the focus upon fixity, upon permanence, upon Being and 'things,' presents problems the moment we attempt to address the awareness with which we are aware of 'things.' If the world is indeed made out of fixed matter, as Cartesian/Newtonian material science determines, then no natural (that is, material) process could possibly give rise to the human minds that experience awareness of such Being. It is a conundrum to which the standard, mainstream scientific answer continues to be essentially that everything is material, and it's only a matter of time before we work out just how a material process can give rise to such an 'apparently' immaterial thing as experiential awareness – the subjectivity which all of us take for granted day by day.

The mind is usually described by such positive scientific approaches as an 'epiphenomenon' of the brain, a nonfunctional supplement that is caused by brain events but has no causal effect upon brain events. It is a curious position: a paradoxical one, even. As Milič Čapek tells us, the scientist who suggests it is saying, in effect, 'I am aware that no awareness exists.'[9] The mind of the human – if it exists at all – is deemed essentially immaterial and wholly unrelated to the world around us. But quite how this squares with a material universe is very difficult to ascertain. After all, 'any interaction between the mental and physical [is] excluded by the laws of classical physics, more specifically, by the laws of conservation of energy and momentum.'[10] If the mind is immaterial, it cannot have any effect upon the material, nor be affected by it. How could anything immaterial, after all, be a cause – in a Newtonian universe – of any material effect? How can we, in other words, decide to do something, and enact anything, if the processes of decision making are immaterial? The equations of classical dynamics would thereby have to invent from thin air energy, or momentum, in the translation between the two: something quite impossible. Worse, the material cannot actually have any effect on the immaterial – no awareness can actually exist – since a physical impact on mind would require the disappearance into immateriality of the energy/momentum of the physical cause.

So the mind must, on the contrary, not be 'epiphenomenal' or immaterial in such a way: it must either not exist at all (but it does – I am thinking!) or be an integral part of the universe if it is to have any effect upon, and be affected, by any of the rest of it. Quite what the mind is, therefore, is the subject of an entire subset of philosophy – the Philosophy of Mind. This contradiction at the heart of modernity has indeed puzzled several great minds, who have sought a way past it, including Spinoza, Bergson, Whitehead, and more recently, Thomas Nagel, among others. Today, many argue, this paradox cries out for resolution.

Process philosophy offers a way out of the conundrum. It offers an understanding of the real that avoids this contradiction by going beyond the distinction between the material and the immaterial. By taking our foot off the brake, as it were, it allows reality to flow once more and to show us that the contradiction arises only if we focus upon fixity. Becoming, in other words, if given primacy over Being, rather than the other way around, and then the two allowed to co-exist in a constant flow, allows us a far more accurate grasp of the real. And not a moment too soon. As Mesle points out, 'process philosophers . . . argue that there is urgency in coming to see the world as a web of interrelated processes of which we are integral parts.'[11] Once the fundamental realisation about the duration of the world is accepted – that it is in the process of becoming, not fixed in the mind of God, that *the future does not exist* but is constantly in the process of becoming, and that all processes are interrelated – the implications of this realisation begin to unfold like a giant ripple across one's entire conception of the universe. If the future does not exist, then *this changes everything.*

Process philosophy becomes, then, 'an effort to think clearly and deeply about the obvious truth that our world and our lives are dynamic, interrelated processes, and to challenge the apparently obvious, but fundamentally mistaken, idea that the world (including ourselves) is made of *things* that exist independently of such relationships.'[12] Fixed, independent things all around us begin to blend into a web of multiple interrelationships that is constantly on the move, shifting, changing, becoming, at every moment poised to go in a range of potential directions, depending on our choices. Even we, of a sudden, thus become a part of this mass of interrelations, no longer the exclusive and independent selves we imagined, but contingent, affected by a host of different influences, and influencing, in turn, all that is around us. A world of individuals engaged with things dissolves into an ongoing dynamic process in which nothing is fixed and everything – and everyone – is interrelated. The primacy of Being over Becoming appears, in the end, quite mistaken: no man is an island, and even islands are connected to everything else if you but look beneath the surface of the waves.

So *the future does not exist*. Three key ideas arise from this realisation: (i) that the subjective, our thoughts, our minds, are more real, and more important – existentially – than some scientific 'epiphenomenality' would suggest; (ii) that time is something other than the measure of moments along a trajectory fixed by an outside entity, like the grooves in a record; and (iii) that our concept of existence as something divided between fixed things and immaterial thoughts is fundamentally in need of revising. I shall now focus a little on each of these three to try to underline how important these realisations are.

The irreversible reality of the subjective

Unfortunately, much of the traditional positive scientific approach outlined in the previous chapter relies upon what contemporary American philosopher Thomas Nagel describes as the 'denial that certain patently real phenomena exist at all.'[13] This applies in many disciplines, including parts of the philosophy of mind, where the influence of a positivist neuroscience strives to be definitive and exclusive (although thankfully there are many exceptions!). In his books *The View from Nowhere* and *Mind and Cosmos*, Nagel shows that the objective stance of many in the philosophy of mind is an 'assumption that what there really is must be understandable in a certain way – that reality is in a narrow sense objective reality.'[14] But such a materialistic approach to the definition of the universe is patently incomplete as a theory of the physical world, 'since the world includes conscious organisms among its most striking occupants.'[15]

Objective reality is defined as the world according to classical physics, a world that is 'superveniently' determined – causally closed – all the way up, by its lowest-level laws. Classical physics is the science, however, as Nagel points out, in which we have achieved 'our greatest detachment from a specifically human perspective on the world.' It is, moreover, 'for precisely that reason physics is bound to leave undescribed the irreducibly subjective character of conscious mental processes, whatever may be their intimate relation to the physical operation of the brain.'[16] As the radical contemporary neuroscientist, Benjamin Libet, stresses, the 'determinist materialist view' that would reduce us to 'a pack of neurons . . . is a belief system; it is not a scientific theory that has been verified by direct tests.'[17] As Nagel points out, such a stance imagines 'we, at this point in history, are in possession of the basic forms of understanding needed to comprehend absolutely anything.'[18]

In contrast, the motivation behind Nagel's and my critique is precisely that I *believe* that the universe is *not* causally closed in this manner and that our subjectivity has a key role to play. There are a number of arguments against causal closure for which there is not the space in this short book to explore. For notions of strong emergence or complex systems, two areas where such causal closure is challenged, I will need to refer the reader to my earlier work, *Bergson, Complexity and Creative Emergence*,[19] where I deal with many of these issues. The 'supervenience' of physical properties, whereby all the higher-level properties of all systems are completely determined by their lower-level properties, is subject both to debate and a good deal of criticism in the philosophy of science literature.[20,21] Most significantly, for our purposes in this book, the key challenge to causal closure lies in the distinction between scientific time and duration: the latter's characteristic is *irreversibility*.

One of Bergson's early interpreters, Jankélévitch, took this idea, implied by Bergson's work, and made much of it. As Lefebvre points out, in *Philosophical Intuition* Bergson 'claims that any great philosopher has, in all honesty, only one or two "infinitely simple" ideas that are elaborated over the course of his or her life.'[22] Jankélévitch's 'big idea,' for Lefebvre, is irreversibility. 'Irreversibility,' he says, in one of his letters, is 'the primitive fact of spiritual life . . . [it is] the very centre of moral life.'[23] I am today no longer the person I was yesterday because the experiences that yesterday brought have changed me. I am today the person whom yesterday changed into me. Tomorrow, likewise, a new me, changed by my experiences today, will emerge. This process of growth is not reversible. More fundamentally, the 'technologies of the self'[24] by which, through my own decision making, I might have choice in the direction in which I change, as a result of today's experience, mean that the person I am today is one in whose creation I have had a hand. This element of choice, moreover, with the self-esteem that can accompany the fulfilment of yesterday's choices today, makes it all the more likely that the person I will be tomorrow will be all the more shaped by the choices I have made in the past. Set, of course, within the web of interrelations, both social and physical, that conspire to determine and circumscribe my freedom, my choices will remain limited, nonetheless, to the 'possible.' At times, where my choices fail, the 'possible' might seem all too constrained. This process of growth, too, is not reversible.

Irreversibility is also a key problem for the causal closure favoured by classical physics. In mechanics, an operation represented in the scientific symbols of measure can flow in either direction. But for this to make sense, Bergson tells us, time must in fact be conceived of as space. It is only by dint of this misconception, crucially, that 'the idea of a reversible series in duration'[25] arises, and in the terms of mathematics and mechanical science, the reversibility of such spatial time seems both inevitable and common-sensical. Yet in conscious terms, as common sense can clearly grasp, if we conceive of time instead in terms of duration, time is not reversible at all, or only in the novels of H. G. Wells.

But classical physics does not have the final say on the matter. In scientific circles, the notion of irreversibility is, in fact, a fundamental property of thermodynamics. Joule's 1847 rule of the conservation of energy offered 19th-century physicists a unification of the whole of nature, which arguably formed the basis of Einstein's later work. But energy conversion, as Prigogine and Stengers point out, 'is merely the destruction of a difference, together with the creation of another difference.'[26] Crucially, in processes where heat is created, it is fuel that is irreversibly destroyed. The process of cooling cannot reconstitute the coal that was burnt. The equivalences in abstract calculations on paper conceal the reality of such destruction. Kelvin, in 1852, once these realisations had set in, understood that the universe was in fact engaged continually and inescapably in such irreversibly destructive processes and formulated the famous Second Law of Thermodynamics: 'the existence in nature of a universal tendency toward the degradation of mechanical energy.'[27] This law, often referred to simply as 'entropy,' in hindsight, was a scientific refutation of the permanent, ideal perpetual-motion machine most scientists at that time conceived the universe to be. The world of Kelvin's tendency to degradation, indeed, is 'an engine in which heat is converted into motion only at the price of some irreversible waste and useless dissipation.'[28]

At the turn of the 20th century, crowning the sweep of classical physics as it had arisen from Newton, Einstein produced relativity theory – but in a universe he conceived as permanent and unchanging. Because of the parallel developments in thermodynamics, however, this Einsteinian universe, as Prigogine and Stengers remind us, published in 1917, was immediately challenged by astrophysicists such as Hubble, whose observations and calculations revealed not a static, but an expanding, universe. 'For many years physicists remained reluctant to accept such an "historical" description of cosmic evolution. Einstein himself was wary of it.'[29] The universe conceived by Einstein and his followers was static – more or less the same throughout eternity – a place where Being had primacy over Becoming. Yet just as looking at the sky had brought about the Newtonian science of classical dynamics in the first place, the irreversibility of time that seems to contradict the balanced order of such a static universe is most apparent in the sky, as we have come to know it since Hubble, where we see all the galaxies of the universe moving farther and farther away from each other, and where there are 'strange objects: quasars, pulsars, galaxies exploding and being torn apart, stars that, we are told, collapse into "black holes" irreversibly devouring everything they manage to ensnare.'[30] The most fundamental implication of the expanding universe, of course, is that the space-time conceived of by Einstein has a history – and therefore a beginning. From this the concept of the Big Bang, and the singularity from which space-time began, emerged. Irreversibility, in short, is absolutely fundamental at the cosmic level.

At the same time, Planck, studying superheated imagined objects known as 'black bodies,' showed that photons – particles of light – behave also like waves. The science of thermodynamics thus spawned quantum physics: a new physics for a new century that made Einstein very uncomfortable. Louis de Broglie, the quantum physicist who showed that *all* particles behave also like waves, in the 1940s looked back on Bergson's late 19th-century work and in it saw the pre-echoes of the realisations of quantum mechanics in the 1920s. The moment you have a wave, you have a duration – a wave unfolds and can only exist in time; matter, in short, in the eyes of the quantum physicists, ceases to be static, and objects cease to be discrete: precisely as Bergson had characterised them. Most fundamentally, these subatomic processes are *irreversible.* Astrophysicists thus proved Einstein's rather Newtonian belief in a reversible simplicity to the universe unfounded, and the quantum theorists such as Planck and Heisenberg then showed how at the microscopic level only probabilities could be adequately described, in a world where not only Newton's, but even Einstein's, theories and equations break down. At issue, in the end, is that a scientifically reversible time, and an experientially irreversible time, are two different things.

How, then, if the neatly mechanical clockwork universe dreamed of in 19th-century classical physics turns out to be rather more complex and unpredictable, are we to understand the world? As Nagel puts it, 'We place ourselves into the world that is to be understood';[31] it is, in short, with our subjectivity that understanding takes place. In this more complex world, moreover, the subjectivity of consciousness is 'an irreducible feature of reality – without which we couldn't do physics or anything else – and it must occupy as fundamental a place in any credible world view as matter, energy, space, time and numbers.'[32]

This is not to suggest – I hasten to add – that if the world is not neatly reducible to the equations of physics and chemistry then it must have been 'intelligently' designed. Again, in Nagel's words, 'those who have seriously criticised these [intelligent design] arguments have certainly shown that there are ways to resist the design conclusion.' Bergson's own approach, in his *Creative Evolution*, is one way such 'finalism' can be refuted at the same time as the 'mechanism' of classical physics. 'But the general force of the negative part of the intelligent design position,' Nagel continues, ' – scepticism about the likelihood of the orthodox reductive view, given the available evidence – does not appear to me to have been destroyed in these exchanges.'[33]

The call of philosophers to recognise the reality of the subjective, in other words, is not a throwback to some pre-modern mythos of a Creator. It is what philosophers do best: they stand back and assess from afar what others too close to their subject tend to miss. 'The existence of conscious minds and their access to the evident truths of ethics and mathematics are among the data that a theory of the world and our place in it has yet to explain.'[34] There are inescapable facts no 'epiphenomenalism' can erase: 'the appearance of living organisms has eventually given rise to consciousness, perception, desire, action, and the formation of both beliefs and intentions on the basis of reasons. If all this has a natural explanation, the possibilities were inherent in the universe long before there was life, and inherent in early life long before the appearance of animals.'[35] Mind, and reason, in other words, must be 'basic aspects of a nonmaterialistic natural order.'[36] Process philosophy, as it has been envisioned first by Bergson and then by Whitehead (though neither named it such) is one approach that tries to recognise this truth.

Bergson's *durée reélle*

Bergson's argument in his famous book, *Matter and Memory*,[37] is about the relation between this subjectivity and the body, and how the answer to this conundrum lies in our understanding of time: that time, indeed, really is something other than the measure of moments along a trajectory fixed by an outside entity, like the grooves in a record. Bergson takes on Descartes' dualism, but seeks to confront it without suggesting a divinely created (or intelligently designed) spirit in man (as Descartes had done, differentiating it and setting it to one side), but suggesting to us, nevertheless, that the profundity of human nature really is beyond what mechanistic science and the positive philosophy of the 19th century could envision.

He contends that previous philosophical approaches to this problem have mostly proposed some vague thesis of union between the two – mind and body – without ever being particularly precise. Ideas current in Bergson's era, he tells us, fall into two categories: parallelism and epiphenomenalism.[38]. Parallelism derived from Dutch radical Enlightenment philosopher Baruch Spinoza. Spinoza (1632–1677) tried to solve the Cartesian impasse in his philosophical and theological treatises, and his posthumously published *Ethics*, opposing Descartes' mind–body dualism, suggested in effect, a third state, of which mind (Thought) and matter (Extension) were the two correlates, two attributes of God as manifest in a united, monist, cosmos. Spinoza's main problem with Cartesian dualism, of course, was that if mind and body are truly distinct, then it is not clear how they can coordinate in any manner. In this third state then, there were, according to Spinoza, direct parallels between everything that is thought and everything that is extension: a mental and a physical half to everything.

Spinoza's ideas were welcomed and lauded as a philosophical grounding for modernity. But his compromise was discarded over the course of the 19th century, with the psychic aspect deemed to accompany only 'some physiological processes in the central nervous systems of higher vertebrates.'[39] Barring such exceptions, the physical universe more broadly was thereby left without any psychic correlates. 'In this way the original universal parallelism of Spinoza was modified in the sense of epiphenomenalism; in the words of Thomas Huxley who coined this term, "The consciousness of higher living beings merely accompanies certain neural processes without influencing them."'[40]

Epiphenomenalism, still perhaps the default, positivist position of many in neuroscience to this day, is thus a degraded version of parallelism, whereby nature has become exclusively mechanical, and only humans (and perhaps one or two other higher vertebrates) exhibit 'mind,' which is deemed to be simply a nonfunctional, almost effervescent supplement, that is caused by electro-chemical brain events, but has no causal effect upon such brain events.

For Bergson neither of these explanations is satisfactory. He certainly believes there is a connection between brain and mental states, but denies that this implies a Spinozan parallelism. Memory, he suggests, is the key to unlocking this problem, as it is situated at the intersection of mind and matter. Contrary to the assumptions of much positivist neuroscience, for Bergson, memory cannot be physical in the way that positive science understands the 'physical.' If so, then much else that goes on in the mind must be similar, and then we have something that is not fixed 'matter,' but which nonetheless is intimately associated with and couples to it. It is in an understanding of the nature of perception and how it relates to memory that Bergson finds an answer.

There have been huge advances in the past century since Bergson, in the relatively 'easy' questions concerning the brain and the cerebral processing of stimuli, leading to a far greater understanding of the relation between brain events and what goes on around the brain than in the 19th century. But the approaches of positivist science have been challenged by what has been found out as this work has unfolded. The assumption, for example, that different parts of the brain are specifically associated with different parts of the body is not necessarily as straightforward as it appears: indeed, it is more probable that the brain is not organised so that each area is responsible for an individual body part, but that different areas are responsible for different functions[41] and that some aspects of our experience seem to have multiple coordinated locations – locations, moreover, which can change over time.[42]

But the question of consciousness, labelled recently as the 'hard problem,' has by contrast, over the last hundred years, been largely side-lined. This 'hard problem,' or, as Chalmers puts it, 'Why is all this [mental] processing accompanied by an experienced inner life?'[43] is something – I would argue – more deservedly at the centre of philosophical debate. The essence of the contemporary debate is whether the 'easy' questions are all you need to answer and whether a 'hard' problem therefore exists at all: whether cerebral processing is all there is, and our experienced inner life is simply a phenomenon 'eliminable' by a completed neuroscience.[44] As we have seen Bergson viewed such 'epiphenomenalism' as insufficient an explanation.

There has been, too, in the 1970s and 1980s, a proposition that our inner experience is some kind of tacit folk psychology or 'theory,' a theory that is long past its sell-by date, and a seriously mistaken theory at that. The proposition argues that this 'theory,' moreover, should be abandoned. This 'theory-theory' proposition is a purely objective approach to subjective realities put forward by a school of thought in contemporary philosophy that I would argue is very thoroughly imprisoned in a lopsided view of the world. Purely objective approaches, such as Churchland's,[45] to subjective realities cannot tell the whole story unless, as these philosophers suggest, subjective realities do not exist. Yet they do exist; I experience them; the assumptions about the world I share with those with whom I am in contact from day to day entail them. This 'theory-theory,' therefore, cannot tell the whole story.

But how did Western philosophy arrive at such a sharp point of denial? For much of the 20th century the 'easy' questions were uppermost in both scientific and philosophical circles. In the early 20th century, behaviourism, or behavioural psychology, stood outside the human (just like Descartes' God) and approached the nature of human behaviour in the manner of cue sticks and cue balls,[46] action and reaction on a collision metaphor without any notion of an inner life – let alone 'choice' – at all. Reacting to this, in the 1950s, cognitivism adopted the new advances in technology with a metaphor for the brain as a digital computer, in which 'mental processes are carried out by the manipulation of symbolic representations in the brain.' Whilst this made meaning, or representational semantics, 'scientifically acceptable,' it was nonetheless 'at the price of banishing consciousness from the science of the mind.'[47] This suggested that the nature of personal awareness amounted merely to 'a few results or epiphenomenal manifestations of subpersonal processing.'[48] Thus beyond a mind–body problem arrived a mind–mind problem, too – the processor mind versus the conscious one. But the digital computer metaphor has been rightly criticised as in fact being situated within a social and cultural phenomenon: the computer is, after all, a processor of social and cultural information and activity, as any interpretivist information systems scholar can tell you. Therefore, a cognitivist model of human cognition can only be 'a model of the operation of a sociocultural system from which the human actor has been removed.'[49]

Connectionism, which followed cognitivism in the 1980s, took as its central metaphor the artificial neural network, emphasising perceptual pattern recognition rather than deductive reasoning. The main problem with connectionism, of course, is that the processing remained enclosed within the brain – contrary to what other philosophers and scientists were beginning to understand was a much more active and environmentally engaged nature of perception and mentality. Connectionism differed from cognitivism mainly in the location of the subpersonal processing of representations: 'symbolic for cognitivists, subsymbolic for connectionists.'[50]

Beyond connectionism and the mindless automatons of 'theory-theory,' work since the late 1980s and into the 21st century has begun to return to the 'hard' problem that the 20th century tried to ignore: How is it that I am conscious? What *is* consciousness? This book, along with others influenced by Bergson and Whitehead's work, joins the assertion of David Chalmers, when he says that we have to 'take consciousness seriously.'[51]

Using the term 'psychical' to describe the conscious – as opposed to 'subpersonal processing' – mind, Bergson distinguishes between perception as a biological and mind as a psychical aspect of our lives. Our psychical life, while bound to its biological motor accompaniment, is, for Bergson, not governed by it.[52] For Bergson, psychical consciousness – the ability to know and to choose – must be quite separate from the more straightforwardly physical nature of perception. Consciousness, for Bergson, must not be physical – susceptible to quantitative measure – at all: it must be a quality, something different in kind.

This is, indeed, the 'hard' problem. Addressing the issue in terms of another classic debate amongst philosophers – between the Real and the Ideal – Bergson quickly establishes the truth of both consciousness and of external reality: if the nerves that convey perception to one's consciousness are cut, it is perception which vanishes, not one's consciousness or the object being perceived. One remains conscious, and the object continues to exist, and these two states remain distinct, but connected. The realist's world of objects, in other words, does exist, but so, too, does the idealist's world of the mind. But for Bergson, the conscious mind is clearly more than just some kind of clever camera, passively receiving a reality that is entirely outside the mind, determined entirely by the outer flow of existence. Recent work supports this dismissal of the photographic approach to understanding perception.[53] On the contrary, for Bergson the richness of the 'inner life' we all experience, and the variety of choice, desire, and agency expressed by it in the ways in which we engage the 'outer' world, makes such a 'realist' position untenable.

This requires us to reimagine reality in terms other than those of the realist and the idealist. Both the body and other objects – all matter, in short – Bergson describes as 'an aggregate of images.' By 'image' he means 'a certain existence which is more than that which the idealist calls a representation, but less than that which the realist calls a thing – an existence placed half-way between the 'thing' and the 'representation.''[54]

Taking this definition of 'images' as a given, Bergson then takes issue with the Idealist's conception that representations of the outside world exist within our minds. For this to be the case, the entire material universe would have to exist in our heads, which it plainly does not. The brain is part of the material universe, not the other way around.

> Itself an image, the body cannot store up images, since it forms a part of the images; and this is why it is a chimerical enterprise to seek to localize past or even present perceptions in the brain: they are not in it; it is the brain that is in them.[55]

As one contemporary philosopher of perception, Alva Noë, puts it:

> we ought to reject the idea – widespread in both philosophy and science – that perception is a process *in the brain* whereby the perceptual system constructs an *internal representation* of the world . . . perception is . . . not a process in the brain, but a kind of skilful activity on the part of the animal as a whole.[56]

Matter, in Bergson's view, is 'the aggregate of images, and perception of matter these same images referred to the eventual action of one particular image, my body.'[57] The most significant 'image' of all, clearly, is our own body, which we perceive both from the outside – for example, looking at our hands – and from the inside – our 'affections,' as he terms it. The body is the 'privileged' image that is both perceived and perceives. The body's perception of the external world, moreover, is directly relevant to what actions are possible: 'The objects which surround my body reflect its possible action upon them.'[58] Cut the nerves that convey this information – as we saw earlier – and the rest of the body, and the external universe, remain, although perception is gone. There is, then, an objective reality outside of the body. Cutting the nerves merely stops the flow of information from the periphery into the brain and back to the periphery, and no more possibilities of action appear. So perception 'is something which concerns action, and action alone.'[59] The body is a centre of action, or, as Bergson stresses, 'indetermination' (i.e., there is choice), 'an object destined to move other objects.' Moreover, because it can perform new actions, the body 'must occupy a privileged position' with regard to other objects.[60] Not mentioning, perhaps unaware of, Bergson, this has been termed recently by Alva Noë the 'enactive approach' to perception.[61] Both the cognitivist metaphor of the mind 'as digital computer' and the connectionist metaphor of the mind 'as neural network' offer 'no account whatsoever of mentality in the sense of subjective experience,'[62] let alone memory, nor indeed 'any sensory and motor coupling with the environment,'[63] as is so obviously clear in the 'enactive' approach.

As neuroscientist Libet puts it, then, a hundred years after Bergson, although it is true that scientific discoveries have produced 'powerful evidence for the ways in which mental abilities, and even the nature of one's personality, are dependent on, and can be controlled by, specific structures and functions of the brain,' it is also undeniable that 'the nonphysical nature of subjective awareness, including the feelings of spirituality, creativity, conscious will, and imagination, is not describable or explainable directly by the physical evidence alone.'[64] The biological and synaptic-electrical arguments concerning spatial, measurable reality that is susceptible to the scientific method, in other words, occur on the mechanical 'outer' to our conscious 'inner.' As Bergson says, 'it is the sensation which is given to us in consciousness, and not this mechanical work.'[65]

So Bergson maintains that the physical apparatus of perception, the nervous system and the brain – the entire body, in fact – is merely this 'centre of action'[66] where perceptions trigger reactions, which in turn trigger movement. Perceived images of the outside world are thereby sketches of potential action. But this purely physical, biological perception–action flow is interrupted by consciousness to enable comparison between several different options and choice between them, before either proceeding or shelving a reaction. The brain is thus an action centre, ready to proceed or shelve a reaction to perceptions. But if perception, linked in this perception–action flow in a biological chain from the external object on the periphery to the action centre in the brain and thereby back through the nervous system into action is essentially physical, a part of the material world, and something which is interrupted by consciousness in order that a choice may be made, what, then, *is* consciousness? For Bergson, it can only be something that is not material, that is different in kind from the matter that it interrupts, albeit but one side of the coin of existence. 'I will not give a definition,' of consciousness, he says in a later essay, 'for that would be less clear than the thing itself; it means, before everything else, memory.'[67] 'Memory' he continues, 'may lack amplitude; it may embrace but a feeble part of the past; it may retain only what is just happening; but memory is there, or there is no consciousness.' All consciousness, then, for Bergson, is memory, the 'conservation and accumulation of the past in the present.'[68]

Using his characteristic supposition of two extremes which do not occur in reality, but whose mixture is better understood if we imagine them, for a moment, apart, Bergson posits two things: pure perception, and pure memory. Pure perception, he argues, is always in the absolute present, existing ultimately outside of us – in the objects that we perceive. Pure memory, by contrast, is entirely in the past. Of course, as Bergson asserts, 'There is no perception which is not full of memories. With the immediate and present data of our senses we mingle a thousand details out of our past experience.'[69] But in order to understand the nature of consciousness and how it relates to perception, Bergson enjoins us to imagine a pure perception and a pure memory.

Now, for Bergson, the sheer quantity of memory would be impossible to somehow store chemically, biologically, within the brain. Most of what we know about memory in scientific circles comes from problems with memory – in particular, cases of brain injury where partial memory loss has resulted. These kinds of experiments and case histories of brain-injured patients were already well underway in the late 19th century, and Bergson uses a great range of such scholarship in his argument. Memory, for Bergson, is not *directly* connected to perceived experience, but exists apart from it, albeit all too often in relation to it. The present – pure perception – is a physical consciousness of the body. The past – pure memory – is an unconsciousness of the body, the realm of fancy and dream.

Memory is that which gives the flow of our perceptions from periphery through the centre to periphery the possibility of choice. We can pause in the centre of action that is our body and compare the motor mechanism action ready to react to our perceptions with previous ones in our memory and weigh up the pros and cons of different outcomes. We may, indeed, choose not to act at all. These separations and distinctions are not absolute, but merely useful: all is, in reality, for Bergson, fluid, interpenetrating. What we actually perceive is always a mixture of the 'pure perception' coming to us from our senses, ready to translate into action, and the images from memory that we project upon the objects we are perceiving, pausing action for the possibility of choice. At this junction, then, between memory, perception, and action, 'the hyphen which joins what has been to what will be,'[70] consciousness acts as a bridge between the past and the future, neither a part of the physical, objective world of perception nor wholly divorced from it in the temporal field of the past; neither wholly physical nor wholly virtual. This is the true extent of the lack of causal closure, of the failure of the supervenience of low-level physical laws: otherwise, they would determine everything, there would be no possibility of choice, no free will, no human preference to interpret – the future, in short, would exist, already predetermined by the past, all the way back to the very beginning of time, and all the way forward to its end. Existence, in short, would be like a recording, played by God over His headphones, and it would make no difference if it took 3 seconds or 30 trillion years to play it.

For Bergson, *the future does not exist*, and consciousness is that which exists in the moment, in the now that links past and future, making choices. Consciousness is not physicality, but the 'now' of physicality, the memory that enables distinction between 'now' and 'then,' and which makes choices regarding what is yet 'to be.' This, like the Cartesian, is a dualistic conception of existence: on the one side matter; on the other consciousness. Yet unlike Descartes, these two – matter and consciousness – are never apart, always indissolubly concurrent and coexistent, and unlike Spinoza, their unity includes a locus of free will not wholly determined by the mathematical rationality of external cause and internal effect. The very moment this dualistic conception of existence is posited, as it were, it is immediately merged into a monistic and moving conception, a unity whereby consciousness *is* matter as it *moves* from the past into the present, and *choice* is located at the verge of potential futures.

This 'moment' Bergson describes as the *durée reélle*. Of all Bergson's core ideas, the *durée reélle* may perhaps be regarded as Bergson's primary insight – the one 'big idea' Lefebvre speaks of, of which irreversibility is but an aspect: an understanding of the nature of time that formed the core of his PhD thesis, later published as his first major book, *Time and Free Will*. In some cases, it is difficult to grasp because, as Bergson would argue, of the many centuries of intellectual thought that have built up describing things in the wrong way. In other cases, it remains common sense, something that we intuitively grasp without recourse to intellect. He reminds the reader of 'the specific feeling of duration which our consciousness has when it does away with convention and habit and gets back to its natural attitude' and enjoins us to remember this understanding of the *durée reélle* as he shows us how 'at the root of most errors in philosophy' one can find precisely this 'confusion between . . . concrete duration and the abstract time which mathematics, physics, and even language and common sense, substitute for it.'[71] This is the core idea of the *durée reélle*: a conception of a continuous reality that is temporo-spatial, in direct contrast to the discontinuous, scientific conception of the spatio-temporal discrete moment that science casts as the real. As Bergson insists, 'succession exists, I am conscious of it; it is a fact.'[72]

One of the principal criticisms levelled at Bergson was that his philosophy – because of its critique of scientific rationalism – was mystical. This criticism was levelled, not only by Bertrand Russell – who wrote a short book critiquing Bergson[73] – but by the Vienna School of 'logical positivists,' who, in the 1920s, held, as we saw in the last chapter, to a strict 'verificationism.' They insisted that any proposition has no factual meaning if no evidence of observation can count for or against it. Many clung to this, as we have seen, even after Gödel had shown in 1931 that the project of reducing all things to logic could not be achieved.[74] That all ethics, aesthetics, and romance, that all (by definition unobservable, unverifiable) subjective experiences are merely meaningless pseudo-statements – eliminable folk psychology – unfortunately continues to be the assumption of some in positive scientific circles and philosophy of mind whose basic approach stems from this period, and the American logical empiricism that followed it when these central European thinkers fled across the Atlantic to escape the ravages of war (e.g. Carnap, Reichenbach, Hempel). This discounting of the subjective – which is clearly wrong – silently underpins so much of what is taken for granted by so many of those applied scientists whose exclusive focus is upon practical application rather than abstract theorising, let alone ontological debate. As we have seen through Ghoshal, Mingers, and others, it is a plain fact that these ideas have impact in the world: immense ramifications, no less. Following the dismissal of Bergson's ideas by these verficationists, many of whom had praised Russell and Whitehead's *Principia Mathematica* (1910), Alfred North Whitehead brought his work with his former PhD student, Bertrand Russell, to a close. There were realisations he could not ignore, realities he could not dismiss. Quietly, in a second career based now in the United States rather than Britain, Whitehead set out to reformulate our concept of Nature.

Whitehead's concept of nature

Turning, then, to our third core realisation, that our concept of existence as something divided between fixed things and immaterial thoughts is fundamentally in need of revising, we come, then, to the work of British mathematician turned philosopher Alfred North Whitehead. The *Principia Mathematica* (1910) was an immensely laudable contribution to the philosophy of logic, but ultimately a failed attempt to found mathematics in philosophy. Unfortunately, in Russell's hands, thereafter, this project, in its second and third volumes, rendered (at least analytic) philosophy – as we saw earlier – the handmaiden to science.

Whitehead, however, understood the implications of the failure of this project. It was, as Mesle points out, simply his misfortune to be 'developing his profoundly new vision of the world just as Anglo-American philosophers were throwing out the metaphysical baby with the bathwater.'[75] In first book in this latter period, *The Concept of Nature* (1920), he acknowledged his debt to Bergson[76] and underlined the unity of a monistic conception of the world. 'For Whitehead,' as Halewood and Michael describe it, 'the aim is to avoid dividing the world into that which is known (external nature) and that which knows (human subjects), and rather to conceptualize and describe nature (in terms of all existence) without recourse to such dualisms.'[77]

What Whitehead protests against, in his work, 'is the bifurcation of nature into two systems of reality.' Both are real, but they are real in different senses. 'Thus,' he continues, 'there would be two natures, one is the conjecture, and the other is the dream.' The way in which we 'bifurcate nature into two divisions' creates a 'nature apprehended in awareness' and a 'nature which is the cause of awareness.' The former, 'apprehended in awareness,' gives us 'the greenness of the trees, the song of the birds, the warmth of the sun, the hardness of the chairs, and the feel of the velvet.' The latter, 'which is the cause of awareness,' is the 'conjectured system of molecules and electrons which so effects the mind as to produce the awareness of apparent nature.'[78] Whitehead sets himself the task of resisting and avoiding all such theories that make nature bifurcate in this way, to approach, as best as he is able, a concept of nature that is monistic, unified, and comprehensive.

For both Bergson, and Whitehead (and incidentally for neuroscientist Libet), as we saw earlier, one of the principal answers to the questions they raise is a reconception of *time* as *duration.* As we have seen, Bergson argues that the idea of a homogeneous and measurable time is an artificial concept, formed by the intrusion of the idea of space into the realm of duration.[79] In the *durée réelle*, he argues, our conscious states are basically qualitative and cannot be adequately described or measured in terms of quantities, and quantities are understood only spatially, and qualities only durationally. Whitehead's approach is similar but subtly different. Rather than distinguishing between quantities and qualities, Whitehead addresses what Bergson described as 'concrete duration,' by focussing upon the notion of the 'event' as a core unit of existence, in a 'structure of events,'[80] but which contains both the physical and nonphysical elements we currently describe in separate ways *as they unfold*. As he describes it, 'What sense-awareness delivers over for knowledge is nature through a period' of time.[81] Using the term by which Bergson's *durée réelle* is most often translated, Whitehead speaks of 'a duration' as 'a concrete slab of nature limited by simultaneity which is an essential factor disclosed in sense-awareness.'[82] This 'duration' is something that is both our subjective experience of an event: a nonphysical consciousness of what is unfolding *and* what the physico-chemical sciences would say about the materiality engaged in the event: the movement of molecules, dynamics of forces, mass, volume and charge of the particles engaged in what is unfolding – the enactive perception of the concrete. The accent, in this notion of the 'event' and the 'structure of events' in which each single event flows, is upon movement: how all is continuously unfolding, changing, never fixed: reality is thus describable only in terms of 'periods' during which conscious and physical interactions and shifts occur. Hence the term 'process' philosophy used to describe Whitehead's approach.

This durational grasp of reality that is at once physical and nonphysical, at once the world as it unfolds and how it is experienced by us, Whitehead characterises as a focus upon the 'event' – often termed by him as 'Actual Occasions' or 'Actual Entities.' Actual Occasions only exist as long as they become, that is, they are to be conceived as a process or as an 'event.' Any 'event,' in this sense, will thus comprise physical and chemical processes as well as personal subjective experience and be part of a 'structure of events' that contain, are contained by, and overlap or interpenetrate it. One example Whitehead uses is that of Cleopatra's Needle: an old piece of rock mounted on a plinth by a river (in this case the Thames, in central London, England), yet steeped in a myriad timelines of history, politics, cultural significance, tourist attraction, graffiti, and the ravages of different eras of pollutants.[83] The Needle is not merely the old bit of North African rock – indeed 'daily it has lost some molecules and gained others'[84] – nor solely any one of the many stories that course around it: it is all these things, and also only those which come to mind as I see it, sitting on the bus crossing the river, on a winter's afternoon, and this experience of the Needle is an 'event' within a 'structure of events,' a 'concrete slab of nature' that includes both the personal and the time it takes to unfold.[85]

The Needle – then, indeed any 'object,' for Whitehead, all matter, in fact – is not 'senseless, valueless, purposeless.'[86] The physical and conceptual (mental) feelings, for Whitehead, always go together, forming two poles within every entity. The physical or conceptual may be of more or less significance in each Actual Occasion, but both are always there. It is their integration, different every time, which makes up what Whitehead calls 'concrescence' – the *process* by which an Actual Occasion, or 'event,' comes to be, becomes, and passes. When the event is over, the Actual Occasion is 'satisfied,' or finished, and, ceasing to be an Actual Occasion any more, it becomes an Objective Datum: it is in the past now and can be studied as such with all the tools of the material sciences. When an Actual Occasion is 'satisfied,' then, it crosses the boundary between Becoming and Being. But once it is an Objective Datum, it is immediately available for the concrescence of new Actual Occasions. Thus, everything is related to everything, for each Actual Occasion must build up a relation, through concrescence, with all the Objective Data in its world. The succession of Actual Occasions makes up time, or the process of duration, as we know and experience it.

The signature uniqueness of Whitehead's approach is that it manages to combine the substance-based theories of time with process-based theories of time (like Bergson's *durée reélle*) into one ongoing conception. On the 'micro level' of concrescence, there are processes, constant change, interrelation; on the 'macro level' of Objective Data, there are enduring objective entities describable and measurable in everyday and in scientific terms.

Whitehead's philosophy, above all, then, represents clear thinking about the role of abstraction in our understanding of and relationship with the world. For Whitehead, we are all too often guilty of imagining our own abstractions to be far more concrete than they actually are. Contemporary society is dominated by abstractions in ways not just philosophers, but all with a social conscience, should heed. As Halewood stresses, using Whitehead's metaphysics as a theoretical grounding for sociological work constitutes 'an investigation of the character and implications of our abstractions' and is not simply 'idle philosophical speculation.' On the contrary, 'It is a vital aspect of the role of theory as a critical diagnostic of contemporary society and social inequalities.'[87] The primary abstractions Whitehead focuses upon, of course, are the dualisms by which we bifurcate the world in our understanding: natural sciences vs. social sciences, objects vs. subjects, reason vs. experience, nature vs. culture, mind vs. body, agency vs. structure, man vs. woman, Being vs. Becoming. All these dualisms are abstractions, and our greatest mistake in trying to understand the universe is to mistake those abstractions for concrete facts. Entire social ills and tragedies are founded upon such fundamental mistakes, which Whitehead describes as the 'Fallacy of Misplaced Concreteness.'[88]

The clarity of Whitehead's analysis here is eye-opening:

> The advantage of confining your attention to a definite group of abstractions, is that you confine your thoughts to clear-cut definite things, with clear-cut definite relations. Accordingly, if you have a logical head,

> you can deduce a variety of conclusions respecting the relationships between these abstract entities. Furthermore, if the abstractions are well-founded, that is to say, if they do not abstract from everything that is important in experience, the scientific thought which confines itself to these abstractions will arrive at a variety of important truths relating to our experience of nature. . . .
>
> The disadvantage of exclusive attention to a group of abstractions, however well-founded, is that, by the nature of the case, you have abstracted from the remainder of things. In so far as the excluded things are important in your experience, your modes of thought are not fitted to deal with them. You cannot think without abstractions; accordingly, it is of the utmost importance to be vigilant in critically revising your *modes* of abstraction. It is here that philosophy finds its niche as essential to the healthy progress of society. It is the critic of abstractions. A civilisation which cannot burst through its current abstractions is doomed to sterility after a very limited period of progress.[89]

Bursting through the abstractions of 19th-century positivism, Whitehead's ontology reconfigures the meanings of 'object' and 'subject,' treating them differently to how we have become used to understanding them. Because for Whitehead all is process and becoming has priority over being, 'subject and object are relative terms'.[90] In other words, each actual entity only exists for as long as it is becoming. It is in this sense a 'subject.' When it has become, it 'perishes.' Of course, in 'perishing,' it does not somehow vanish from the universe. Rather, it becomes a potential item of data for the creation of new entities. In this sense, it is an 'object.' In this manner, the processual interrelated flow of the universe is not undifferentiated. The connectivity of the universe does not cancel out the distinctiveness of individual entities. Rather, each 'becoming' unfolds in its own distinctive manner, incorporating different elements from every other becoming. Every kaleidoscopic pattern of the possible is a unique one. It is, moreover, *how* it becomes that makes it not just unique but what it *is*. Whitehead thereby manages to combine both the differentiation of individual concrete things in the world with a fundamental interrelatedness and connectivity of them all, in the way that they come to be, the way that the universe unfolds. For Whitehead, too, in other words, *the future does not exist*.

Process-relational philosophy today for information systems

Bergson's influence, despite his eclipse in the 1930s, in fact shows through in much of later French philosophy. Deleuze may be the only one to acknowledge it, but Bergson's influence is clear throughout poststructuralist thought, as I have argued elsewhere.[91] Whitehead's insights can be found not just underpinning, but acknowledged as foundational by some of the key writers on contemporary critical theory. Latour acknowledges him, and by implication the work of such thinkers as Dolphijn and van der Tuin,[92] Barad,[93] and Winner,[94] and their 'New Materialism' and 'agential realism,' all find their roots in Whitehead's attempt to go beyond bifurcation.

Crucially, Whitehead's ideas are not as far from the understandings an information systems scholar reading this short book might imagine, either. They sit, in fact, at the foundation of Actor Network Theory. This theory, for anyone not familiar with it, can be introduced simply through the archetypal illustration from Latour,[95] who describes the problem of getting hotel guests to leave their keys behind. This is a scenario of use about how to inscribe a desired pattern of behaviour into a network composed of hotel guests, keys, and staff. In Latour's story, the hotel management first tried to instil the desired behaviour by means of a sign behind the counter requesting guests return their room keys. They then employed a doorkeeper to verbally remind guests as they left the building. Finally, they inscribed the aim into a key with a metal fob, the size and weight of which was gradually increased until the desired behaviour was finally achieved. In his work, then, Latour is making the point that humans live in a world of objects[96] and that these objects are supplemental neither to human life nor to a proper understanding of it. Like Whitehead, Latour is saying that 'to separate these into two realms (that of the social scientist and that of the natural scientist) is both to confuse and over-simplify the complexity of existence.[97,98] Nor is this philosophical foundation to Actor Network Theory by chance. As Halewood and Michael point out, 'Latour uses the work of Whitehead to support and develop his arguments[99,100,101] – principally in his book, *Pandora*, but also in journal papers[102] and lectures[103] and a review he wrote of Stengers' book on Whitehead.[104] Other writers[105] have also made the link, one asserting that Whitehead's 'relational view of space might now be seen as the dominant paradigm within human geography and in many ways ANT is quite congruent with this general shift in thinking across human geography.'[106]

I believe it is time that the information systems community that is engaged with ANT more thoroughly addressed the material-relational foundations of Actor Network Theory in Whitehead's philosophy.

Notes

1 Mesle, R.C. (2008) *Process-Relational Philosophy*. West Conshohocken, PA: Templeton Press, pp. 4–5.
2 Perry, R.B. (1935) *The Thought and Character of William James*. Boston: Little, Brown, Volume 2, pp. 622–623 https://archive.org/details/thoughtandcharac032117mbp

3 Whitehead, A.N. (1920/2007) *The Concept of Nature*. New York, NY: Cosimo, p. 54.
4 Mesle, R.C. (2008) *Process-Relational Philosophy*. West Conshohocken, PA: Templeton Press, p. 7.
5 ibid., p. 8.
6 ibid., p. 6.
7 ibid., pp. 8–9.
8 Latour, B. (1993) *We Have Never Been Modern*. Edinburgh: Pearson.
9 Capek, M. (1987) 'Bergson's Theory of the Mind-Brain Relation' in *Bergson and Modern Thought*, Papanicolaou, A. and Gunter, P. (eds.), p. 130. Chur: Harwood Academic Publishers.
10 ibid.
11 Mesle, R.C. (2008) *Process-Relational Philosophy*. West Conshohocken, PA: Templeton Press, p. 9.
12 ibid., p. 8.
13 Nagel, T. (1986) *The View from Nowhere*. Oxford: Oxford University Press, p. 7.
14 ibid.
15 Nagel, T. (2012) *Mind and Cosmos*. Oxford: Oxford University Press, p. 45.
16 Nagel, T. (1986) *The View from Nowhere*. Oxford: Oxford University Press, p. 7.
17 Libet, B. (2005) *Mind Time: The Temporal Factor in Consciousness*. Cambridge, MA: Harvard University Press, p. 5.
18 Nagel, T. (1986) *The View from Nowhere*. Oxford: Oxford University Press, p. 10.
19 Kreps, D. (2015) *Bergson, Complexity and Creative Emergence*. London: Palgrave.
20 Cartwright, N. (1999) *The Dappled World*. Cambridge: Cambridge University Press.
21 Skrbina, D. (2007) *Panpsychism in the West*. Cambridge, MA: MIT Press.
22 Bergson, H. (1946) *The Creative Mind*. Translated by M.L. Andison. New York: Philosophical Library, p. 128.
23 Lefebvre, A. (2015) 'Introduction' in Jankélévitch, V. *Henri Bergson*, Lefebvre, A. and Schott, N. (eds.), p. xv. London: Duke University Press.
24 Foucault, M. (1988) 'Technologies of the Self' in *Technologies of the Self: A Seminar with Michel Foucault*, Martin, L., Gutman, H., and Hutton, P. (eds.). Amherst: University of Massachusetts Press.
25 Bergson, H. (1889/2005) *Time and Free Will*. Adamant Media Elibron Classics Reproduction of 1913 edition translated by F.L. Pogson. New York: George Allen and Unwin, p. 102.
26 Prigogine, I., and Stengers, I. (1984) *Order Out of Chaos*. London: Flamingo, p. 111.
27 ibid., p. 115.
28 ibid.
29 ibid., p. 215.
30 ibid.
31 Nagel, T. (1986) *The View from Nowhere*. Oxford: Oxford University Press, p. 4.
32 ibid., pp. 7–8.
33 Nagel, T. (2012) *Mind and Cosmos*. Oxford: Oxford University Press, p. 11.
34 ibid., p. 31.
35 ibid., p. 32.
36 ibid.
37 Bergson, H. (1908/2004) *Matter and Memory*. Mineola, NY: Dover.
38 ibid., p. x.

39 Capek, M. (1987) 'Bergson's Theory of the Mind-Brain Relation' in *Bergson and Modern Thought*, Papanicolaou, A. and Gunter, P. (eds.), p. 133. Chur: Harwood Academic Publishers.
40 ibid.
41 Kikkert, S., Kolasinski, J., Jbabdi, S., Tracey, I., Beckmann, C., Johansen-Berg, H., and Makin, T. (2016) 'Revealing the Neural Fingerprints of a Missing Hand' *eLife* 5, p. e15292.
42 Greenfield, S. (2000) *Brain Story*. London: BBC.
43 Chalmers, D.J. (1996) *The Conscious Mind.* Oxford: Oxford University Press, p. xii.
44 Churchland, P.M. (1981) 'Eliminative Materialism and the Propositional Attitudes' *Journal of Philosophy* 78(2), pp. 67–90.
45 ibid.
46 Juarrero, A. (2002) *Dynamics in Action: Intentional Behaviour as a Complex System*. London: MIT Press, p. 3.
47 Thompson, E. (2007) *Mind in Life: Biology, Phenomenology, and the Sciences of Mind.* London: Belknap Harvard, p. 5.
48 ibid., p. 6.
49 Hutchins, E. (1995) *Cognition in the Wild.* Cambridge, MA: MIT Press, p. 363.
50 Thompson, E. (2007) *Mind in Life: Biology, Phenomenology, and the Sciences of Mind.* London: Belknap Harvard, p. 10.
51 Chalmers, D.J. (1996) *The Conscious Mind.* Oxford: Oxford University Press, p. xiii.
52 Bergson, H. (1908/2004) *Matter and Memory*. Mineola, NY: Dover, p. 83.
53 Noë, A. (2006) *Action in Perception.* London: MIT Press, pp. 35–72.
54 Bergson, H. (1908/2004) *Matter and Memory*. Mineola, NY: Dover, p. 7.
55 ibid., p. 196.
56 Noë, A. (2006) *Action in Perception.* London: MIT Press, p. 2.
57 Bergson, H. (1908/2004) *Matter and Memory*. Mineola, NY: Dover, p. 7.
58 ibid.
59 ibid.
60 ibid., p. 5.
61 Noë, A. (2006) *Action in Perception.* London: MIT Press, p. 75.
62 Thompson, E. (2007) *Mind in Life: Biology, Phenomenology, and the Sciences of Mind.* London: Belknap Harvard, p. 6.
63 ibid., p. 9.
64 Libet, B. (2005) *Mind Time: The Temporal Factor in Consciousness*. Cambridge, MA: Harvard University Press, p. 5.
65 Bergson, H. (1889/2005) *Time and Free Will.* Adamant Media Elibron Classics Reproduction of 1913 edition translated by F.L. Pogson. New York: George Allen and Unwin, p. 7.
66 Bergson, H. (1908/2004) *Matter and Memory*. Mineola, NY: Dover, p. 5.
67 Bergson, H. (1920/1975) *Mind-Energy*. Translated by H. Wildon Carr. Westport, CT: Greenwood Press, p. 7.
68 ibid., p. 8.
69 Bergson, H. (1908/2004) *Matter and Memory*. Mineola, NY: Dover, p. 24.
70 Bergson, H. (1920/1975) *Mind-Energy*. Translated by H. Wildon Carr. Westport, CT: Greenwood Press, p. 9.
71 Bergson, H. (1889/2005) *Time and Free Will.* Adamant Media Elibron Classics Reproduction of 1913 edition translated by F.L. Pogson. New York: George Allen and Unwin, p. vii.

72 Bergson, H. (1907/1944) *Creative Evolution.* Translated by A. Mitchell, with a Foreword by I. Edman. New York: Random House Modern Library, p. 368.
73 Russell, B. (1977) *The Philosophy of Bergson.* Folcroft, PA: Folcroft Library Editions.
74 Kleene, S. (1967/2001) *Mathematical Logic*. London: John Wiley, p. 250.
75 Mesle, R.C. (2008) *Process-Relational Philosophy*. West Conshohocken, PA: Templeton Press, p. 4.
76 Whitehead, A.N. (1920/2007) *The Concept of Nature*. New York, NY: Cosimo, p. 54.
77 Halewood, M., and Michael, M. (2008) 'Being a Sociologist and Becoming a Whiteheadian: Toward a Concrescent Methodology' *Theory, Culture & Society* 25(4), p. 32.
78 Whitehead, A.N. (1920/2007) *The Concept of Nature*. New York, NY: Cosimo, pp. 29–31.
79 Bergson, H. (1889/2005) *Time and Free Will*. Adamant Media Elibron Classics Reproduction of 1913 edition translated by F.L. Pogson. New York: George Allen and Unwin; Boland, R. (2001) 'The Tyranny of Space in Organizational Analysis' *Information and Organisation* 11, pp. 3–23.
Kreps, D. (2015) *Bergson, Complexity and Creative Emergence*. London: Palgrave.
80 Whitehead, A.N. (1920/2007) *The Concept of Nature*. New York, NY: Cosimo, p. 52.
81 ibid., p. 57.
82 ibid., p. 53.
83 'Cleopatra's Needle' is in fact the name given to three such obelisks, the other two being in Paris and in New York, carved at different periods of the ancient Egyptian civilization, but none having anything to do with the famous late Pharaoh Cleopatra. Paris gained the first in 1826, London the second in 1877, and New York the third in 1881. https://en.wikipedia.org/wiki/Cleopatra%27s_Needle
84 Whitehead, A.N. (1920/2007) *The Concept of Nature*. New York, NY: Cosimo, p. 167.
85 ibid., p. 53.
86 Whitehead, A.N. (1926/1932) *Science and the Modern World.* New York: The Free Press, Simon and Schuster, p. 17.
87 Halewood, M. (2008) 'Introduction to Special Section on A.N. Whitehead' *Theory, Culture & Society* 25(4), p. 4.
88 Whitehead, A.N. (1926/1932) *Science and the Modern World.* New York: The Free Press, Simon and Schuster, p. 58.
89 ibid., pp. 58–59.
90 Whitehead, A.N. (1933/1967) *Adventures of Ideas*. New York: The Free Press, Simon and Schuster, p. 176.
91 Kreps, D. (2016) 'An Encounter between Gramsci, Marx, Foucault and Bergson' *2nd International Conference on Cultural Political Economy: Putting Culture in Its Place in Political Economy*. Bristol University, Bristol, UK, 25th–26th August 2016.
92 Dolphijn, R., and Van der Tuin, I. (2012) *New Materialism: Interviews and Cartographies*. Ann Arbor, MI: Open Humanities Press.
93 Barad, K. (2007) *Meeting the Universe Halfway*. Durham, UK: Duke University Press.
94 Winner, L. (1986) *The Whale and the Reactor: A Search for Limits in an Age of High Technology*. Chicago: University of Chicago Press.

95 Latour, B. (1991) 'Technology Is Society Made Durable' in *A Sociology of Monsters: Essays on Power, Technology and Domination*, Law, J. (ed.), pp. 103–131. London: Routledge.
96 Latour, B. (1993) *We Have Never Been Modern*. Hemel Hempstead: Harvester Wheatsheaf, pp. 142–145.
97 ibid., pp. 51–55.
98 Halewood, M., and Michael, M. (2008) 'Being a Sociologist and Becoming a Whiteheadian: Toward a Concrescent Methodology' *Theory, Culture & Society* 25(4), p. 32.
99 Latour, B. (1999) *Pandora's Hope: Essays on the Reality of Science Studies*. Cambridge, MA: Harvard University Press, pp. 141, 153, 305, 306.
100 Latour, B. (2004) *Politics of Nature: How to Bring the Sciences into Democracy*. Cambridge, MA: Harvard University Press.
101 Halewood, M., and Michael, M. (2008) 'Being a Sociologist and Becoming a Whiteheadian: Toward a Concrescent Methodology' *Theory, Culture & Society* 25(4), p. 33.
102 Latour, B. (2007) 'La connaissance est-elle un mode d'existence ? Rencontre au Muséum de James, Fleck et Whitehead avec des fossiles de chevaux' in *The Handbook of Science and Technology Studies*, Hackett, E., Amsterdamska, O., Lynch, M., and Wacjman, J. (eds.), (3rd ed.), pp. 83–112. Cambridge, MA: MIT Press.
103 Latour, B. (2008) 'What Is the Style of Matters of Concern? Two Lectures in Empirical Philosophy' *Spinoza Lectures at the University of Amsterdam, April and May 2005*. Published as an independent pamphlet, Van Gorcum, Amsterdam.
104 Latour, B. (2005) 'What Is Given in Experience? A Review of Isabelle Stengers "Penser Avec Whitehead"' *Boundary 2* 32(1), pp. 222–237.
105 Debaise, D. (2013) 'A Philosophy of Interstices: Thinking Subjects and Societies from Whitehead's Philosophy' *Subjectivity* 6, p. 101 https://doi.org/10.1057/sub.2012.24
106 Murdoch, J. (1998) 'The Spaces of Actor-Network Theory' *Geoforum* 29(4), p. 359.

4 The world in a new light

Introduction

If the thrust of process philosophy as explored in the last chapter holds true, then many of the fundamental problems in the world today can be seen as being a direct or indirect result of the false philosophy of bifurcation, fixity, and the reification of abstractions. Being – with all the isolation and focus upon the individual that it entails – must, if we are to address these problems, be seen as secondary to Becoming, with all the connection, interrelatedness, and collectivity that it implies. Choices – and as human beings in a process-relational world our choices are fundamental and constitutive – become a great deal clearer, between positivism and interpretivism, between accents upon individualism and collectivism, and between reductionism and complexity.

If everything – and everyone – is interrelated in a collective flow, the philosophy and methodology of individualism can be regarded not only as a false emphasis but as actually harmful, severing ties and bonds, dependencies and co-requisites upon which good health depends. Positivism, built as it is upon methodological individualism, seen in the light of process philosophy, becomes a danger to personal psychological balance – cutting us off from one another; a danger to the social fabric – undermining and impoverishing our civic life; and a danger to the ecological health of the planet – ignoring the (eco)systemic impact of our activities upon everything around us in the natural world. The possessive quality of individualism at the heart of the neoliberal project of the past decades, let us recall, not only conceives the individual as the proprietor of his or her own person and capacities, *but that she or he owes nothing to society for them*. This assault upon the public sphere, and the resulting growth in inequalities where this socio-economic philosophy is strongest,[1] can be seen as directly counter to a process-relational understanding of the world.

In the digital sphere, if this positivist methodological individualism embedded in our computer and information sciences is harmful, then an education focussed upon it to the exclusion of the humanities must indeed produce generations of damaged individuals.[2] The 'nerd' of the 1980s became the 'geek' of the 1990s, and the 'digital native' of the new century. 'Alone Together,' as Sherry Turkle describes them,[3] the millennial generation have grown up with a connectivity that is mediated by computer systems built upon a philosophy that treats each of us as a rational, selfish island and discounts our humanity as 'meaningless pseudostatements.' Digital transformation seeks only profit in a zero-sum game already won by a handful of billionaires whose platforms are tearing down the international peace.[4] These and other ramifications and choices are explored in this chapter.

Implications for IS

Acknowledging the Bergsonian backdrop to Foucault's critique of scientific rationalism[5] and Whitehead's ontological underpinning of Actor Network Theory and the New Materialism, a critical information systems scholar is ready to explore and embrace process philosophy. But what sort of impact is this likely to have?

As Klein and Myers point out, interpretivism already acknowledges that IS are a process:

> as Parmenides observed, 'you cannot swim in the same river twice.' Interpretivists argue that organizations are not static and that the relationships between people, organizations, and technology are not fixed but constantly changing. As a consequence, interpretive research seeks to understand a moving target.[6]

In other words, information systems must be seen as dynamic, subject to continual change – in ways even faster and more profound than perhaps Klein and Myers were implying. A reconception of the nature of Nature, informed by Bergson and Whitehead, as a starting point, not only sets aside the positivist bifurcation of nature enjoining us to adopt a more critical path in IS, but in so doing 'repersonalises,' for want of a better word, or redeems from its positivist lifelessness, the natural world around us. Our sense awareness, in Whitehead's terms, is reconnected to 'the greenness of the trees, the song of the birds, the warmth of the sun,' from which a focus upon the 'the conjectured system of molecules and electrons' has, as scientists, divorced us.[7]

This reconnection to the natural world is, moreover, closely linked to the interest in social change already prevalent in critical IS. A reconceptualisation of nature in line with Bergson and Whitehead, acknowledging, with Nagel, the reality of subjectivity and placing it within a structure of scientific understanding within a durational frame, would constitute a reunification of our concept of nature that could bring a halt to our destruction of our environment and, in the narrower context of IS, could help IS scholars and practitioners to critique, rework, and design better systems that incorporate all of reality: the IT and the people who use and change it and the natural world we live within. Process-relational philosophy implies a shift away from positivism in IS.

Individualism in a new light

IS scholars do not – although some would perhaps prefer to – live in a bubble. Information has become the blood of the body politic, the thread of the social fabric, the breath of our social lives, and the calculus of our economies. The systems through which it flows are constitutive, determining, and foundational. Those who make them must look up from their screens and embrace the significance of their work for society at large. Computing – at least as it is traditionally configured – is focussed upon the discrete, and when it deals with people it deals with them as individuals, not as individual parts of a wider collective, of a society. This has to change.

Systemic individualism

What I will term systemic individualism is a social condition affecting societies. It is a condition of societies that have seriously begun to lose, or have already lost, the glue that truly holds a society together, the glue that makes it a society, rather than a mere aggregate of individuals. In that sense, a society in which a particular brand of individualism has taken such root as to become systemic is a failing or failed society, whose internal systems, channelling the interactions of those within it, have become governed by a contradictory ethic: rules for interaction within a collective based upon a philosophy that denounces any collectivity; rules for interaction within a society that believes 'there is no such thing' as society, 'merely individual men and women and. . . . families.'[8] The United Kingdom and the United States are two societies where systemic individualism has taken hold increasingly since the 1970s. Other countries have experienced similar shifts, but I will focus here on the UK and on the United States.

In societies with this condition, the economic and social or cultural infrastructure – those things 'held in common' – have been subject to a different ethic: they either never have been held in common (e.g. health care in the United States) or having been (re)built and maintained by the public purse have been sold by the state to corporations and individuals in the belief that their management will be more efficient if driven by the profit motive and governed by the 'market' (e.g. the privatisation programme of the last several decades in many Western societies and in societies unfortunate enough to have had to turn for financial assistance to global financial bodies that required neoliberal restructuring as the price of their assistance).[9]

The condition of systemic individualism is the outcome of individuals arguing for a specific kind of individualism to become a governing ethic within societies. This kind of individualism is Nozickian.[10] It is an individualism in which individuals *owe nothing to society.*[11] It rests on an 'atomistic view of society as a mere aggregate of individuals.'[12] Those arguing for it are arguing for a world that justifies their own desire to take and to have what they want without regard or responsibility to anyone else. This is the sense in which those arguing for this individualism define 'freedom.' But this 'freedom' is more an immaturity lacking responsibility for those around one and looking only to the advancement and interests of oneself.[13] It is a 'freedom' that denies the interrelatedness we have seen, in the previous chapter, that lies at the heart of reality itself. It is a creed that says that people should have the right to take what they want, when they want it, without regard to the needs or wants of others. It is an alienating ideology, which pushes people away from each other, each to stand alone in their own 'kingdom,' free to do as they please – with *nothing held in common.*

The philosopher Thomas Hobbes, in keeping with the ideas that were at the time giving birth to the scientific method, 'reduced the world to its analytic components of individual self-interest and built it up again from this single base,'[14] with the claim that a universal, irreconcilable conflict lay at the heart of human society that could only be held back through the might of a governing sovereign. The notion of a self-interestedly rational individual as a social unit thus took root in the minds of some thinkers at the time and soon gained ground. Locke's individualism, some centuries later, as we saw earlier, was heavily concerned with ensuring the new breed of English capitalists could 'grab' – before anyone else – as much of the New World as possible for themselves and specifically without monarchical or aristocratic interference. Locke was thereby both regalising the individual – making him (*sic*) sovereign over his own holdings – and incorporating a legitimate role for self-interest into democratic theory: if the poor did not have the vote (as another theorist, Colonel Rainborough, put it at the time), 'the rich would "crush" them.'[15] The vote, in this sense, rather than partaking in collective governance for mutual benefit, became simply a means of protecting one's interests – especially if you're a 'first grabber' intent on protecting your appropriated possessions. Individualism in the United States, as a result, is foundational, a part of the cultural glue that holds

American society – loosely – together: the famous American Dream. The fall of the British Empire over the course of the 20th century and the rise of the United States as a global power to fill the gap have also seen the spread of this very ideology to every corner of the world. The United Kingdom, moreover, linked culturally and linguistically to its former colony as much as financially, has been engaged in recent decades in the same 'neoliberal' project more than any other. Since the publication of Nozick's *Anarchy, State and Utopia* in 1974,[16] in both the United States and the UK, this cult of individualism has become *systemic*, and the effect upon the fabric of society has been marked. As the International Monetary Fund politely put it in their shocking paper, 'Neoliberalism: Oversold,' in 2016, 'The evidence of the economic damage from inequality suggests that policymakers should be more open to redistribution than they are.'[17] It is clear from Picketty's work that a reversal from a narrowing to an increasing income gap between rich and poor took place in 1979.[18]

Individualism, in short, in light of process-relational philosophy, clearly runs counter to the reality of the world. It is, as this entire book has been attempting to state, *against nature*; not just our own nature, as individualities inescapably interdependent upon one another, but against the natural world of which we are a part.

The tech giants and the cyber war

Meanwhile, in the world of discourse, as Thomas Kuhn[19] so memorably showed, the charisma of individual scientists and their paradigmatic sway over their discipline lends support to their 'truth,' while they do their best to starve alternatives of funds, exposure, and institutional credence. Here, a methodological individualism is embedded in the very roots of the scientific method, as we have seen in our discussion of positivism, and was so clear in the development of Darwin's Adam Smith–style 'natural selection.' This methodological individualism and the self-owning first-grabbers of market-fundamentalist individualist capitalism are, of course, very closely aligned. Science is, after all, as one critic put it, 'politics by other means,'[20] and some of the most famous scientists in history were also entrepreneurs,[21] charismatic individuals who closed down dissent whilst promoting their theories.[22] Today is no different – or, rather, under the yoke of neoliberalism, in many parts of the world, it is more marked than ever before. The great technology inventers and entrepreneurs of our day are also multibillionaires. According to Oxfam, the world's eight richest people (that *Forbes* knows about)[23] collectively own 50% of the world's wealth (calculated by Credit Suisse Global Wealth Databook 2016).[24] Let's pause a moment to state that again: eight of the seven and a half billion people alive in 2018 own half of all the wealth owned by all of the people alive. Symptomatic of individualism is that these stupefyingly wealthy men (yes, of course they are all men) almost certainly do not trust one another, let alone act in concert unless they deem that each of them stands, individually, to gain.

In the 20th century, the encroachment of neoliberal individualism coincided with the rise of the computer. The resulting computerisation of administration, both private and public, has incorporated the methodological individualism of positivist scientific approaches into companies, corporations, and public institutions. This is a 'perfect storm': the combination of (i) possessive individualism in political theory; (ii) methodological individualism in scientific rationalism; (iii) methodological individualism applied to philosophy and social science; (iv) methodological individualism applied to the economic theory promulgated in business schools and pursued in government policies, and thereby into the structuring of our economies; (v) the development, at the height of scientific rationalism in the mid-20th century, of the foundations of computing; and (vi) the progressive expansion of computing, through the phenomenon of disruption, into becoming an all-encompassing processor of social and cultural information and activity – which it packages for sale. Methodological individualism, in other words, has become a defining characteristic of our daily lives: a *systemic individualism*.

Computer science and information systems, as taught in our schools and universities and as represented in the technology-focussed media, are disciplines that are all too often heavily biased towards a positivistic outlook upon the world, one which regards the 'humanities' as woolly airy-fairy pursuits with no practical value. This division between the sciences and the arts has rendered the latter as of lesser importance – in contrast to the 19th-century education that so valued the classics, alongside the sciences. Today, subjects like political theory, ethics, and the emotional education to be derived from literature and drama, the understanding of perspectives different from one's own available through foreign languages, history, and art, are all lesser cousins to the industrial necessities such as maths, physics, chemistry, biology, engineering, computing, and the character and fitness building of competitive sport which prepare us for the market.

The individuals, then, at the helm of the tech giants – those technology companies that have ridden the tidal wave of disruption that has swept the efficiency of computerisation into every corner of our lives – these individuals have, all too often, received an education that has simply not prepared them for the sway that they now hold over so many millions of lives. As one journalist describing this phenomenon points out: 'What is intriguing about the Facebook founder is his astonishing blend of high intelligence, naivety and hubris.'[25] All traits, I would argue, developed by a lopsided education.

The tech giants – Facebook, Google, Twitter, etc. – have built astonishingly sophisticated tools for harvesting our personal information and the trails of data we leave across the Internet. These tools, in the background, then refine this information ready for sale to (any and all) advertisers in 'high-speed data-trading auctions that are entirely unregulated and opaque to everyone except the companies themselves.'[26]

Now all this has been challenged by a few interpretivist and critical information systems academics,[27] but has not surfaced into public discussion until the events of 2016: the referendum on EU membership in the UK, and the election of Donald Trump as president of the United States. These events and the spotlight of investigative journalism (notably Carole Cadwalladr in *The Observer* and its sister paper *The Guardian*) that then turned upon the tech giants has brought to light another – far murkier – story that the advertising platforms (Google, Facebook, etc.) have brought us: the cyber war allegedly being waged across the planet, principally by Russia, and by a range of secretive billionaires, whose interests have merged: destabilisation, it seems, serves the purposes both of a Russian foreign policy seeking room for manoeuvre, and of multi-billionaire Machiavellian princes who either simply profit from volatility[28,29,30,31,32,33] or whose fanatical religious allegiances are directly promoting Armageddon.[34] Needless to say, Russia denies any such involvement, as do the billionaires Carole Cadwalladr implicates. Standing back, from a philosophical perspective, the withdrawal of the UK from the EU and the victory of an 'America First' agenda in the United States are simply the peak of the systemic individualism gripping both countries, outlined earlier.

The two nations – the United States[35] and UK[36] – where inequality is at its worst across the planet (according to The World Top Incomes database), and where the political project of possessive individualism and the scientific rationale of methodological individualism are at their strongest – the so-called Anglo-American model,[37] have thus been successfully persuaded – with help from the highly sophisticated advertising engines of social media – to permanently diminish their global reputation,[38,39] stimulate a bonanza of lucrative market volatility,[40] and arguably place the evangelical agenda of the 'End of Days' into US foreign policy,[41] whilst handing the reins of the UK government to a clique seemingly bent on realising the ultimate dream of an already tarnished neoliberalism: turning the whole of the UK into a tax haven on the shores of Europe.[42]

Such foreign policy and billionaire agendas have been around for a long time, of course. What the naïve and hubristic tech giants have given them, however, for Carole Cadwalladr and other investigative journalists focussing on these events, is the tools with which to achieve their aims.[43] As an article in *Vanity Fair* pointed out recently, there are early Facebook employees publicly regretting the 'Monster' they created.[44] The fallout, indeed, from the events of 2016, when Facebook was allegedly used as a platform for this cyber war, has led one early Facebook employee to tell us that he lies 'awake at night thinking about all the things we built in the early days and what we could have done to avoid the product being used this way.'[45] Another – a former vice-president of user growth, no less – recently declared: 'social media is ripping society apart' and expressed his deep regret for his part in building tools that destroy 'the social fabric.'[46] He said, 'The short-term, dopamine-driven feedback loops that we have created are destroying how society works. No civil discourse, no cooperation, misinformation, mistruth.'[47] Even Zuckerberg, Facebook's founder and CEO, mindful of the reputational damage of all these revelations, has 'asked forgiveness after admitting that his work has been used to "divide people." '[48]

Eric Schmidt, the man behind Google, has said the previous approach of the technology industry to misinformation had been 'naïve' and that

> almost all the things in [Google] and the other tech companies can be understood as the maturation of what we do. Ten years ago, I thought that everyone would be able to deal with the internet because the internet, as we all knew, was full of falsehoods as well as truths. But faced with the data, from what we've seen from Russia in 2016 and with other actors around the world, we have to act.[49]

Facebook, thereafter, have also admitted they were too slow to recognise and react to 'Russian election interference.'[50]

Looked at a little deeper, perhaps Marshall McLuhan was right: 'The medium is the message,'[51] he said, and the message shapes us. The ICTs deployed by the tech giants materialise atomising social structures as they impose them, and those social structures are neoliberal in the extreme. Facebook, as one *Columbia Journalism Review* author put it, is 'Eating the World.' 'Social media' she tells us, 'hasn't just swallowed journalism, it has swallowed everything. It has swallowed political campaigns, banking systems, personal histories, the leisure industry, retail, even government and security. The phone in our pocket is our portal to the world.'[52] Moreover, Facebook in particular, for all the rhetoric of 'connecting people,' is fundamentally a 'tangle of rules and procedures for sorting information, rules devised by the corporation for the ultimate benefit of the corporation. Facebook is always surveilling users, always auditing them, using them as lab rats in its behavioural experiments.'[53] The social media platform 'paternalistically nudges users in the direction it deems best for them, which also happens to be the direction that gets them thoroughly addicted.'[54] The platform is a medium, of course, but for what? For generating advertising leads in the cleverest targeted advertising machine ever conceived – hence its phenomenal capital valuation. The message carried by that medium, therefore, turns every user into a product for sale to those purchasing advertising – whether commercial or political. Facebook's founding president, Sean Parker, who became a billionaire thanks to the company, recently said: 'God only knows what it's doing to our children's brains.' Speaking at an event in Philadelphia, he said the founders of the social media giant 'knew they were creating something addictive that exploited "a vulnerability in human psychology"'[55] from the outset. Zuckerberg, of course, was supposed to be majoring in psychology at Harvard, though he 'mostly took computer science classes until he started Facebook and dropped out.'[56]

Once a process-relational philosophical perspective has been adopted and we can see how all is interconnected, interrelated, and unfolding in a world where *the future does not exist*, the immensely powerful medium of social media can be seen in a new light. As set out in my paper in 2010,[57] the online profiles of social media can best be understood as masks rather than as representations of a 'fixed' self. In the end, as we all continuously grow and change, continuously impinging upon one another's development, there are only masks, and no such 'thing' as a fixed self to represent. Social media's worst impact, perhaps, has been to localise self-worth and self-esteem within such profiles for those (inevitably young) people whose wealth of experience has many years yet to accumulate the robustness of more stable character (not a fixed self, more a set of developed tendencies). Measuring one's self-worth by the number of 'likes' one receives for a status, these young people have been persuaded by these information systems to take something momentary, fleeting, 'in the moment,' and place it – eternally, forever to be found again – as a Facebook status or Tweet from which they will never escape, fixing their thought permanently, nailing them down to the past, requiring that they answer today for their stance of yesteryear. The right to be forgotten[58] – newly introduced in EU law – seems all too Cnut-like, sweeping back the tide, in the face of the power of the tech giants. That genuine crimes of the past should be answered for does not mean that every utterance should be perpetually held against one.

Social media platforms need to flow from well-thought-through objectives in our collective best interest, not according to the greed or machinations of a powerful few. The fixity and data retention of such systems is only for the benefit of marketing intelligence. What is transitory should remain transitory. Above all, social media platforms need to be democratised – from the code up – not monopolised by the half-educated and naïve tech entrepreneurs whose neoliberal agendas belie their protestations of radicalism.

Above all, the technology creatives in this new world need humane and lifelong learning, not the by-rote schooling of positivist classrooms.

Implications for ecology: this changes everything

The implications for the natural world, meanwhile, of the individualism of the past centuries, have been devastating. Not only was 2015 the hottest year since records began in 1880, but it was the 16th in a row of the 16 warmest years ever recorded, all since 1998. It was also, thanks to the efforts of those trying to avert disaster, finally, the first year in which global CO_2 emissions stopped increasing.[59] But the story of the scientific endeavour that has researched, measured, and brought to our attention and demanded action on climate change – which changes everything[60] – is one that is just as damning of early 20th-century positivism and methodological individualism, in the crucible of which the earliest forms of the science of ecology were forged.

It took a complete revolution in scientific understanding – and a good deal of fieldwork observation – for a new generation of ecologists to realise that the formulaic models created in the 1950s and 1960s simply did not match the reality. Daniel Botkin's 1992 work, *Discordant Harmonies*, proved to be one of the most seminal works in environmental biology in recent decades. One of its most striking aspects was his assertion that the individualism of 19th-century approaches to evolution is a red herring. As I pointed out in Chapter 2, Darwin's own original understanding was to focus upon species, rather than individuals, but with the prevailing methodological individualism of the 19th century he felt he had no choice but to try – like Adam Smith – to 'understand the whole in terms of the individual parts and their interactions.'[61] As Botkin asserts, however, this doesn't add up in ecological terms:

> Individuals are alive, but an individual cannot sustain life. Life is sustained only by a group of organisms of many species – not simply a horde or mob, but a certain kind of system composed of many individuals of different species – and their environment, making together a network of living and non-living parts that can maintain the flow of energy and the cycling of chemical elements that, in turn, support life.[62]

In other words, a kind of actor network.

Ecosystems, indeed, by the end of the 1990s, had begun to be understood in a very different way to the mathematicised approaches of Hutchinson, Lindemann, and the Odum brothers and their irradiated Pacific atolls. Their symbolic, quasi-algebraic language used to represent and calculate the behaviour of species, resting on the cybernetic principles of self-regulation and feedback tending back toward equilibrium and rest, once finally subjected to rigorous and exhausting fieldwork in the wild, proved, in the end, to bear little resemblance to actual natural processes at all. Until Botkin, the predominant theories in ecology 'either presumed, or had as a necessary consequence a very strict concept of a highly structured, ordered, and regulated, steady-state ecological system.'[63] Botkin exposed how this view is simply wrong at both local and regional levels and at the levels both of populations and of ecosystems. 'Change,' he stressed, 'now appears to be intrinsic and natural at many scales of time and space in the biosphere.'[64] Indeed, as the work of Kauffman,[65] Jablonka and Lamb,[66] Oyama et. al.,[67] Pibliucci and Muller,[68] and others, have underlined in the 25 years since Botkin's *Discordant Harmonies*, it's all a lot more *complex* than that. Botkin's new *nonequilibrium* ecology soon gathered a huge following, breaking with the old positivist approach, and a complex adaptive systems approach, where order spontaneously arises at the edge of chaos, has become a core understanding in the life sciences.

Fundamental to an understanding of *living* systems, then, has been the relatively new science of complex adaptive systems, or its very closely related field, complexity theory. One of the most famous writers on the subject, contemporary with Stuart Kauffman, was physicist Murray Gell-Mann, whose book, *The Quark and the Jaguar*, explored the relationship between the simple and the complex. The simple refers to 'underlying physical laws of matter and the universe,' which Gell-Mann asserts are quantum-mechanical. Therefore, since quantum mechanics 'supplies only probabilities for alternative coarse-grained histories,'[69] chance must play a role in the unfolding of the universe. The future, in other words, does not exist. The field combines ecology, physics, economics, chaos theory, and contemporary revised versions of a more complex cybernetics that feed into artificial intelligence (AI).

Information systems, in their traditional positivist mode, made no allowance for complexity. In the same manner that equilibrium ecology insisted on a structured, ordered steady-state that is simply not reflected in the real world, so positivist information systems made no allowance for the problems of 'real managers,' as we saw in Chapter 2. Yet the recent burgeoning of AI is built, in some respects, upon these very new understandings – specifically in the form of artificial neural networks, whose principles are closer to complex adaptive systems than the simple feedback loops of 1950s cybernetics.

There is little space in this short polemical book to explore the intricacies of complexity theory, nor for the finer issues surrounding the deployment of AI in the old, methodologically individualist context of social media, where it is being used to understand our all-too-human behaviour better than ever before. However, two key examples will suffice to suggest that a process-relational philosophical approach is much more in harmony with complexity than it ever was with reductionism: (i) dissipative structures – a key concept in nonequilibrium ecology – and (ii) a necessarily very brief introduction to network dynamics.

Dissipative structures

A straightforward image by which to grasp the nature of dissipative structures is to picture, for a moment, a tap, from which running water pours into a bath. As it flows down through the plughole it forms – spontaneously – a whirlpool or vortex: this is a dissipative structure. The vortex exists only in the nonequilibrium condition of the flow of water, taking the matter of the water and the energy of its flow in from the tap and passing it on down the plughole. At the site of its structure, however, the order and organisation of the water molecules makes the spiral of the vortex. This ordering of the water molecules cannot be derived or imputed from the molecules that make up the whirlpool, nor the forces of attraction or repulsion between those molecules. The order comes from the external environmental conditions – the flow of the water from tap to plughole. The composition of the liquid flowing from the tap is irrelevant. Such unpredictable open systems exist in conditions far from equilibrium: not only is the system not at rest, but, on the contrary, has a good deal of both matter and energy passing constantly through it, as with the flow from tap to plughole. The order of the dissipative structure, moreover, emerges as a part of this flow, conditioned by the macroscopic parameters, and not by its constituent parts.[70]

Species, ecosystems, the entire biosphere may be characterised as 'dissipative structures,' through which the flow of energy and the cycling of chemical elements that support life take place. That a study of the individual alone, or the processes associated only with individuals, could tell us all there is to understand about such vast interpenetrating systems is no longer tenable. Their behaviour, like that of the flow of water from tap to plughole, actually often has little to do with that of the individual components – the molecules of water; it is in many cases more a macroscopic property of their collectivity, of the energy and unfolding of their durational flow from past to present to future. Contemporary ecology, then, concentrates as much upon those wider systems as upon individual organisms, with an added understanding that dynamic adaptive complexities are the principal characteristics of those systems, especially in the interplay between them, and that methodological individualism in science, as well as in politics, has had its day. The implication, of course, is that the balance between structure and agency, between collectivism and individualism, in social organisation must be sought out anew, and work is ongoing amongst sociologists to try to map the complexities of social structures using these new techniques.[71]

Network dynamics

Complex systems often incorporate fundamental transitions from multiplicity to unity – from chaos to order. There is, in short, a kind of 'invisible hand,' but which works in ways Adam Smith did not clearly understand. A simple, conceptual explanation of this process is offered by Kauffman describing what he calls a 'phase transition,' involving buttons and threads:

> Imagine 10,000 buttons scattered on a hardwood floor. Randomly choose two buttons and connect them with a thread. Now put this pair down and randomly choose two more buttons, pick them up, and connect them with a thread. As you continue to do this, at first you will almost certainly pick up buttons that you have not picked up before. After a while, however, you are more likely to pick at random a pair of buttons and find that you have already chosen one of the pair. So when you tie a thread between the two newly chosen buttons, you will find three buttons tied together. In short, as you continue to choose random pairs of buttons to connect with a thread, after a while the buttons start becoming interconnected into larger clusters. . . . A phase transition occurs when the ratio of threads to buttons passes 0.5. At that point, a 'giant cluster' suddenly forms . . . [as] most of the clusters have become cross-connected into one giant structure.[72]

Such network dynamics, moreover, occur in electrical, chemical, and biological conditions. Stuart Kauffman, in 1971, (building on work in the late 1960s on genetic nets)[73] made a connection between molecular systems and network dynamics in the inaugural issue of the *Journal of Cybernetics*.[74] In this paper Kauffman described how a single chemical reaction can be described as autocatalytic if the product of the reaction is also the catalyst for that reaction. A set of such 'circular' chemical reactions can be described as 'collectively autocatalytic' if at least some of those reactions produce catalysts for enough of the other reactions so that the entire set of chemical reactions is self-sustaining, given sufficient input of energy and food molecules. This is known as an autocatalytic set.

Such autocatalytic systems occur, not just in laboratory dishes with a mixture of organic chemicals, but amongst single-celled organisms – for example, the amoebas in cellular slime mould.[75] A very primitive life form, cellular slime mould has two distinct phases to its life cycle. Whilst food in the form of bacteria is available, the amoebas of the slime mould exist as independent single cells, crawling about seeking and consuming food. As single-celled organisms, their reproduction consists in growth and division, and during this phase they seem to pay little, if any, attention to one another. Their behaviour changes radically in the second phase of their cycle. When the food runs out, the amoebas start to communicate with one another, releasing chemical signals that take messages from cell to cell. The first release of the chemical creates a centre to which cells receiving the signal start to move, themselves releasing a burst of the chemical as they gather. This aggregation, moreover, then gradually morphs into a multicellular organism:

> [T]he initially simple aggregate of cells becomes progressively more complex in form, and the cells in different positions differentiate into specific cell types. The final structure consists of a base, a stalk that rises up from the base, and on top a 'fruiting body' made up of a spherical mass of spores that can survive the absence of food and water. When conditions recur that allow growth, the spores are released from the fruiting body and germinate – each one producing an amoeba that feeds, grows, and divides – and the life cycle starts again.[76]

What is taking place in this shift from a mere aggregation of independent amoebas to a purposeful multicellular organism? Clearly there are organic chemical reactions underway that generate transformations, but also there seems to be a fundamental transition from multiplicity to unity – from chaos to order. The network dynamical laws reviewed here that give rise to complex behaviour are more than just initial conditions from which one can deduce the resulting complex behaviours, as some theorists have suggested.[77] On the contrary, the very openness of these systems results in a complexity that counters the chaos that would otherwise ensue: downward causation, in short, is taking place, achieving simplicity – order – out of the chaos. Thus, a picture of the 'simplicity' that we see around us as being, far from simple rules one can 'reduce' everything to, but a delicate homeostatic balance on the very edge of chaos, begins to emerge, suggesting that the old reductive, positivist scientific approach is very much missing the point. Indeed, the fundamental problem with positivist thought when applied to complex systems is that to represent a complex system one must, of necessity, reproduce the system in its entirety. The representation, usually something like an algorithm – the 'shortest description' which can capture the essential elements of a system – can only capture the entirety of a complex system because a complex system is already its own shortest description. In computation, this is known as an 'incompressible algorithm.'[78] As another great complexity theorist, Rosen, put it, ‘a system is *simple* to the extent that a single description suffices to account for our interactions with the system; it is *complex* to the extent that this fails to be true.’[79] In other words, when a single (dynamical) description is capable of successfully modelling a system, then the behaviours of that system can, by definition, always be correctly predicted. But such a system will not be complex, in that there will not be any unanticipated behaviours. By contrast, systems that require multiple partial dynamical descriptions – no one of which, or combination of which, is enough to successfully describe the system – are complex. The result of this is that truly complex systems are only susceptible to a collection of partial descriptions which may overlap but do not collectively cover all the gaps. As Rosen puts it, complex systems ‘appear to possess a multitude of partial dynamical descriptions, which cannot be combined into one single description.’[80] Cartwright’s *Dapple World* comes once more to mind.

Following on from the work of Botkin, Goodwin, and Kaufmann, an entire field of enquiry opened up, with its own journal, *Ecological Complexity*, and foundational books such as by May,[81] Allen and Starr,[82] and Maurer,[83] along with the magnificent work that is ongoing at the Santa Fe Institute[84] which explores all of complexity theory, not just the ecological kind. Recent work by Jablonka and Lamb,[85] Pigliucci and Muller,[86] Juarrero,[87] Thompson,[88] and Oyama et al.,[89] all push these ideas further than there is space to devote to them in this necessarily short volume.

New understandings of how ecology actually works in sum are very much in keeping with a process-relational philosophy and are quite contrary to a methodological individualist positivist approach. Everything is indeed connected and in delicate balances, inhabitants co-evolving with the habitats around them. For all the homeostasis that enables flexibility, such order-at-the-edge-of-chaos nonequilibrium ecosystems can, if pushed too far, moreover, go careering off a tipping point towards a completely new balance, and one that may not be much of a home for any of us.

Ecological imperialism

Now the global ecological system really is as delicate as any tiny system a complexity biologist might study in a laboratory. We, as a species, have already completely remade our planet, and we are responsible for maintaining it. The clearest example I can give is not the oldest nor the most recent. Every day, at pretty much every meal, every person on the planet experiences the changes we have wrought upon the ecology of our planetary home over the last 500 years, since Columbus arrived in the New World. The Columbian Exchange, as it is known, which followed has completely changed the world – from the soil upwards.

Briefly, as introduced by Alfred Crosby in his ground-breaking 1972 work, *The Columbian Exchange: Biological and Cultural Consequence of 1492*,[90] and supported by his later *Ecological Imperialism: The Biological Expansion of Europe, 900–1900*,[91] and by Grove's equally celebrated book, *Green Imperialism: Colonial Expansion, Tropical Island Edens and the Origins of Environmentalism 1600–1860*,[92] the immense terraforming that has been underway since the colonial expansion of the European powers is quite mind-boggling.

The arrival of the Europeans in America was a shock to both. Native American inhabitants, the First Nations, had been living in isolation for tens of thousands of years. So 'when Columbus brought the two halves of this planet together,' the native inhabitants met their 'most hideous enemy: not the white man nor his black servant, but the invisible killers which those men brought in their blood and breath.'[93] The fatal diseases of the Old World were more effective killers in the New World, and comparatively benign diseases of the Old World became fatal in the New. There is written evidence of 14 epidemics in Mexico and 17 epidemics in Peru between 1520 and 1600.[94] Only when those most susceptible to the new diseases had already died and some interbreeding had introduced immunity into the local population did numbers begin to recover. Although population numbers prior to the arrival of the Europeans are exceedingly difficult to estimate, perhaps some 90% of the indigenous populations of the Americas died from disease by the end of the 17th century.[95] Crosby's work on this disease-driven aspect of population dynamics is regarded to this day as a 'classic.'[96]

Millions of Europeans, meanwhile, in Crosby's tale of the 17th century, began to emigrate across the Atlantic, replacing the indigenous populations that were dying out. Key to enticing them to make the journey, however, was the availability of familiar foods. Indeed,

> the successful exploitation of the New World by these people depended on their ability to Europeanise the flora and fauna of the New World. That transformation was well underway by 1500, and it was irrevocable in both [N]orth and South America by 1550.[97]

This change was so fundamental, moreover, that 'in this matter, as in that of diseases, the impact of the old world on the new was so great that we of the 20th century can only imagine what pre-Colombian America must've been like.'[98]

A key difference between the Old and New Worlds, however, meant that this transformation of the New World into the Old World was by no means one way. Large mammals were almost nowhere to be found across the Americas. This was most likely due to the impact of human settlement.

These same humans, however, with little meat to eat as a result, had turned their skills and innovation to the creation of some of the most nutritious plants available anywhere on the planet.

When they first arrived, and thereafter in certain climates where the Old World crops simply would not take hold, the European settlers had to eat local food. 'Manioc or cassava . . . quickly became the staple of the diet in Brazil . . . The Spanish always preferred wheat to maize bread, but could not always obtain or afford it.'[99] A host of other local foods, however, were happily adopted. Pumpkins and beans became common on settlers' tables. Settlers in America, as with people at home in Europe, 'were very slow to accept potatoes as a staple food,'[100] but, eventually, it became more popular – even too popular, as the potato blight famine in Ireland in the 19th century was to show.

The statistics on global population growth in the post–Columbian era are testimony – in Crosby's thesis – to the efficacy and sheer nutritiousness of these Native American plants. As Crosby said in 1972, 'In the last 300 years the number of human beings on this planet has quadrupled, doubling between 1650 and 1850 and then once again in the last century.'[101] There were 6 billion inhabitants of planet Earth in 1972. As I write there are more than 7.5 billion, and all indicators point to over 9 billion by 2050.[102] As Crosby notes, 'It is provocative to those engaged in an examination of the biological consequences of the voyages of Columbus and his generation to note that this population growth has occurred since 1492.'[103] McKeown's thesis held that improved nutrition was key to population growth,[104] and it is generally accepted that world population has grown continuously since the Great Famine and Black Death of the mid-14th century.[105] Crosby's thesis suggests that the natural recovery of the population after these events then received, at the close of the 15th century, an exceptional boost. Countering other arguments for this expansion, Crosby settles on the increase and improvement of the food supply as the key cause and links this to the world-wide spread of the highly nutritious Native American staples so carefully cultivated by the meatless Neolithic Native Americans. The list is impressive (all but three of the listed names here, moreover, are derived from Native American words):

- Maize
- Pumpkin
- Beans of many kinds (*Phaseolus vulgaris* and others)
- Papaya
- Guava
- Peanuts
- Avocado

- Potato
- Pineapple
- Sweet potato
- Tomato
- Manioc (also called cassava and tapioca)
- Chile pepper (*Capsicum annuum* and others)
- Squashes
- Cocoa

So, 'driven by the fact that America provided so few domesticated animals for food, the [Native American] produced some of the most important of all food plants'[106] for the entire world. Collectively, moreover, 'these plants made the most valuable single addition to the food producing plants of the old world since the beginnings of agriculture.'[107] The staples, in particular, upon which the world today depends, are, in large measure, from America. Using figures from the Food and Agricultural Organization Yearbook 1963, Crosby showed that the Old World crops provided some 22.1 million calories per hectare at that time – rice 7.3, wheat 4.2, barley 5.1, and oats 5.5. By contrast American crops – maize 7.3, potatoes 7.5, sweet potatoes and yams 7.1, and manioc 9.9 – were providing 31.8 million calories per hectare. The quality of American staples, then, in terms of calorie yield, is clear.[108]

Now, European colonists, for Crosby, in his later work, 'were seldom masters of the biological changes they triggered' in the New World, and though they 'benefited from the great majority of these changes,' their role 'was less often a matter of judgment and choice than of being downstream of a bursting dam.'[109] This is to depict human history as at the mercy of ecological forces, tantamount to an 'ecological determinism'[110] I would not sign up to, being more of a mind that a good deal more human impetus was involved. Arguably, as we have grown in number, the climatic and ecological influences upon our population have diminished and our social choices increased. As Barry Cunliffe has ably shown in his work on the prehistory of Eurasia, although climatic influences and the ecological niches of particular plants later to be domesticated play a crucial role, the

> gregarious nature of the human species and its predilection for reproduction led, inevitably, to a growth in population and the emergence of larger social groups. These imperatives within human society, played out against a changing climate, created the tense dynamic that nurtured the transition to settled agriculture[111]

which then itself boosted human population growth. In other words, human history has seen many such population expansions, and although it is always a mixture of climatic, ecological, and human social influences that is at play, the latter has been crucial from the start, and gaining in importance. The reverse impact, moreover, of human population growth upon both the ecological and climatic conditions of the planet has also been growing.

The behaviour of the Columbian Exchange was evident again when Europeans arrived, some centuries later, in Australasia. Any visit to New Zealand, in particular, will impress one how much like Wales it has become, covered in Old World grass and sheep, both introduced by European settlers.[112,113] The tiny patches left of the Kauri forests that covered half of New Zealand – after most of these magnificent trees became ships' masts and spars in the late 19th century – offer a last glimpse of what was once a strikingly different landscape.

We live, therefore, today in a world of our own making. There can be no doubt about this. There is nowhere else, moreover – but other planets – for us to go. Whether the impulses that brought about the Neolithic, the more recent possessive and methodological individualism, or simply the greed of European powers intent on empire are at fault, the Colombian Exchange grants us undeniable evidence of our capacity to remake our environment to a point which we completely and blindly take for granted, and with an impact that is quite incalculable. The effect we, as a species, have had upon the world, moreover, has not only been getting more and more fundamental, but it is happening faster and faster. The scale of the impact of our activities on the delicate global ecosystem, moreover, is only now coming to light.

Ecological breakdown

This short book is not the place to rehearse the evidence for anthropogenic climate change, and we will take the evidence for this as read. At least one famous pundit in the world of ecological warnings, however – George Monbiot – has come to describe our current predicament, no longer as 'climate change,' but as 'climate breakdown.'[114] The horrific problems seem to mount up by the day. Beyond the ever-worsening global temperature increases, there are a host of other issues facing the world today. Two in particular, for me, stand out.

First, the way we treat the land. The more than 75% decline over 27 years in total flying insect biomass in protected areas – research published in *PLOS One* in October 2017,[115] reported in the broadsheet media,[116] and dubbed 'Insectageddon' by Monbiot[117] – shows that modern intensive farming methods threaten not just the global population of flying insects, but everything that depends upon them. The 'erasure of non-human life from the land by farming,' as Monbiot describes it, is leading not just to the collapse of wild animal and bird populations, but to a decline in productivity on 20% of the world's cropland.[118] The industrial agricultural practices that ignore how the area of each field is closely interrelated with the surrounding ecology – methodological individualism in agriculture[119,120] – are the cause of the problem. 'The volume of pesticides and the destruction of habitat have turned farmland into a wildlife desert'[121] and are thereby beginning to reduce its capacity to produce food. There is even growing evidence that climate change itself is having a deleterious effect on the nutritional value of the food we eat.[122,123,124,125]

There is enough food for everyone on the planet to be well-fed. A United Nations report only a few years ago summed up the problem of unequal food distribution very well:

> World average per capita availability of food for direct human consumption, after allowing for waste, animal-feed and non-food uses, improved to 2,770 kcal/person/day in 2005/2007. Thus, in principle, there is sufficient global aggregate food for nearly everyone to be well-fed. Yet this has not happened: some 2.3 billion people live in countries with under 2,500 kcal, and some 0.5 billion in countries with less than 2,000 kcal, while at the other extreme some 1.9 billion are in countries consuming more than 3,000 kcal.[126]

The problems of malnourishment and obesity are, in short, related through global economic inequality. But the impact of intensive farming in the countries where consumption is dangerously high and in countries where all too much of the food is exported is part of a wider global mass extinction event, beyond Insectageddon.[127] As the International Panel on Climate Change (IPCC) documents put it in 2007: 'There is high confidence that climate change will result in extinction of many species and reduction in the diversity of ecosystems.'[128] By 2015 there was little doubt, with new research revealing 'an exceptionally rapid loss of biodiversity over the last few centuries, indicating that a sixth mass extinction is already under way.'[129]

Second, the way we treat the sea. The horrific problem of overfishing has seen the nine biggest fishing companies in the world voluntarily join forces to try to prevent it.[130] The overall health of the oceans, meanwhile, is under attack from several different directions. The warming of the oceans over the past decades is now more accurately understood than ever before[131] – and is far worse than previously thought. Such warming brings not just the increased likelihood of devastating storms, as we have seen in recent hurricane seasons (2017 not the deadliest, but, along with 2005's Katrina, one of the costliest hurricane seasons since 1926),[132] but also the loss of biodiversity in seas where the CO_2 used to go (some 150 billion tonnes of it since the Industrial Revolution),[133] but which just can't absorb much more. Ocean acidification, as it is known, because CO_2 in the salt water turns into carbonic acid – thankfully in tiny quantities – has proven sufficient to raise seawater from what is normally a slightly 'basic' or pH >7, to pH-neutral. At pH-neutral, moreover, less sulphur evaporates from the sea into the air as part of the water cycle, making the surface of the oceans less reflective and more absorptive of sunlight, further increasing the warming of the oceans. The acidification and warming of the oceans are proving catastrophic for a whole range of different ocean ecosystems, not just the coral bleaching caused by unusually high temperatures, but permanent changes in populations of plankton in certain areas and large-scale migrations of fish populations towards the poles.[134]

As if all this weren't enough, the problem of plastic pollution has also risen recently to the fore, revealing what a devastating impact our wastefulness is having upon the seas. There are plastic fibres now coming out of our tap water[135] around the world,[136] let alone floating on the surface of the sea. Pictures of the '[t]ide of plastic rubbish discovered floating off idyllic Caribbean island coastline'[137] that were shared in the media during the autumn of 2017 were just the latest evidence of the growing problem of plastic pollution. Microplastics, the invisible plastic dust cousins to the fizzy drinks bottles gathered on the surface, are perhaps an even greater problem – a threat to the marine ecosystem and to human health, according to one recent paper.[138]

Process-relational radicalism

The atomistic view of society as a mere aggregate of individuals in short, promoted by Locke, lauded by Nozick, built into our economies and institutions by the atomising rationale of all too many computerised administration systems, infecting our relationships through their mediation by smartphones 'connecting' us through the social media platforms that treat us as advertising targets, and have unwittingly exposed us to the cyber warfare of the power-hungry, the greedy, and the plain crazy – this sociopathic condition of systemic individualism – is destabilising the climate which has enabled us to succeed as a species in the first place.

The methodological focus upon fixity, upon Being – with all the isolation and individualism that it entails – must, if we are to even begin to address all these problems, be seen as secondary to Becoming, with all the connection, interrelatedness, and collectivity that it implies. In IS it is clear that positivism must be challenged and pushed aside from its ascendancy in the field, giving way to an interpretive focus that conjoins the IT with the people who make it, use it, affect it, and are affected by it. Systemic individualism must be redressed – quickly – by new modes of working together: not some monolithic (and equally positivist) Soviet approach, that attempts to erase individuality altogether, nor a path that merely glosses the individualism of the neoliberal agenda with charitable good works by which the rich can feel better about their wealth. It is not beyond the wit of man – or of professional political philosophers – to work out a far better distributive justice than is currently the norm without erasing the incentives that enable some to get (a little) ahead of the rest – but no further than the conscience of the collective should allow. The digital revolution destabilising our former settlement must be regarded as an opportunity for a thorough rethinking of how we manage our societies – not for a precious few to become a new aristocracy. The tech giants, motivated by their founding radicalism, should stop being the distraction engines that facilitate such 'land grabs' of vast wealth and power and work toward social empowerment. As AI becomes more and more important in the workings of our systems, the structural implications of complexity should become more and more important. We cannot any longer simply trust to systems founded around individuals alone to ensure that we are collectively moving in a direction beneficial to all. It clearly does not work. The rights of the collective must be enshrined in our laws as well as the rights of the individual.[139] Above all, such a new *conscience* about our fellows must also extend to a conscience about the world we live in, an inclusion of the rights of the planet's well-being in our calculations of cost and benefit. I propose not some Jainist fear of causing harm to any life, but I am not the only one who knows – even as I today eat my steak – that to survive we must all, in due course, become vegetarian, if not vegan.[140] The logistics of meat production are today perhaps one of the single most wasteful and inefficient burdens upon the environment of our bloated population. We must treat the land and sea as good husbandmen and husbandwomen, and as good societies. Our economic freedom to do as we wish with what we own must be curtailed by our responsibilities to the rights and freedoms of those around us – including the health and well-being of the flora and fauna with whom we share this planet.

Notes

1 The World Wealth and Income Database http://wid.world/

2 Naughton, J. (2017) 'How a Half-Educated Tech Elite Delivered Us into Chaos' *The Guardian* www.theguardian.com/commentisfree/2017/nov/19/how-tech-leaders-delivered-us-into-evil-john-naughton

3 Turkle, S. (2011) *Alone Together*. Philadelphia, PA: Basic Books.

4 Cadwalladr, C. (2016) 'Google, Democracy and the Truth about Internet Search: Tech-Savvy Rightwingers Have Been Able to "Game' the Algorithms of Internet Giants and Create a New Reality Where Hitler Is a Good Guy, Jews Are Evil and . . . Donald Trump Becomes President' *The Observer* www.theguardian.com/technology/2016/dec/04/google-democracy-truth-internet-search-facebook

5 Kreps, D. (2016) 'An Encounter between Gramsci, Marx, Foucault and Bergson' *2nd International Conference on Cultural Political Economy: Putting Culture in Its Place in Political Economy*. Bristol University, Bristol, UK, 25th–26th August 2016.
6 Klein, H.K., and Myers, M.D. (1999) 'A Set of Principles for Conducting and Evaluating Interpretive Field Studies in Information Systems' *MIS Quarterly* 23(1), p. 73.
7 Whitehead, A.N. (1920/2007) *The Concept of Nature*. New York, NY: Cosimo, pp. 29–31.
8 Margaret Thatcher, *Woman's Own*, 31 October 1987 www.margaretthatcher.org/document/106689
9 Ostry, J.D., Loungani, P., and Furceri, D. (2016) Neoliberalism: Oversold? www.imf.org/external/pubs/ft/fandd/2016/06/pdf/ostry.pdf
10 Nozick, R. (1974) *Anarchy, State and Utopia*. Oxford: Blackwell.
11 Cohen, G.A. (1995) *Self-Ownership, Freedom and Equality*. Cambridge: Cambridge University Press.
12 Floridi, L. (2017) 'Infraethics – on the Conditions of Possibility of Morality' *Philosophy of Technology*. Editor Letter https://doi.org/10.1007/s13347-017-0291-1
13 Mansbridge, J. (1990) *Beyond Self-Interest*. Chicago: University of Chicago Press.
14 ibid., p. 4.
15 ibid., p. 5.
16 Nozick, R. (1974) *Anarchy, State and Utopia*. Oxford: Blackwell.
17 Ostry, J.D., Loungani, P., and Furceri, D. (2016) Neoliberalism: Oversold?, p. 41 www.imf.org/external/pubs/ft/fandd/2016/06/pdf/ostry.pdf
18 Picketty, T., and Goldhammer, A. (2014) *Capital in the 21st Century*. Cambridge, MA: Harvard University Press.
19 Kuhn, T. (1970) *The Structure of Scientific Revolutions*. Chicago: University of Chicago Press.
20 Winner, L. (1986) *The Whale and the Reactor: A Search for Limits in an Age of High Technology*. Chicago: University of Chicago Press.
21 Take the case of Edison, as described by Carlson, W.B. (1992) 'Artifacts and Frames of Meaning: Thomas A. Edison, His Managers, and the Cultural Construction of Motion Pictures' in *Shaping Technology/Building Society*, Bijker, W. and Law, J. (eds.), p. 177. Cambridge, MA: MIT Press.
22 For example geologist Charles Lyell, as described by Schweber, S.S. (1977) 'The Origin of the *Origin* Revisited' *Journal of the History of Biology* 10(2), p. 252*n*.
23 Withnall, A. (2016) 'Vladimir Putin "Corruption": Five Things We Learned about the Russian President's Secret Wealth' *The Independent* www.independent.co.uk/news/people/vladimir-putin-corruption-five-things-we-learned-about-the-russian-presidents-secret-wealth-a6834171.html
24 Hardoon, D. (2017) *An Economy for the 99%: It's Time to Build a Human Economy That Benefits Everyone, Not Just the Privileged Few*. Oxfam https://policy-practice.oxfam.org.uk/publications/an-economy-for-the-99-its-time-to-build-a-human-economy-that-benefits-everyone-620170
25 Naughton, J. (2017) 'Why Facebook Is in a Hole over Data Mining' *The Guardian* www.theguardian.com/commentisfree/2017/oct/08/facebook-zuckerberg-in-a-hole-data-mining-business-model
26 ibid.
27 Zuboff, S. (2015) 'Big Other: Surveillance Capitalism and the Prospects of an Information Civilization' *Journal of Information Technology* 30(1), pp. 75–89.

28 Vanbergen, G. (2017) How Brexit Was Engineered by Foreign Billionaires to Bring about Economic Chaos – for Profit http://truepublica.org.uk/contributor-news/how-brexit-was-engineered-by-foreign-billionaires-to-bring-about-economic-chaos-for-profit/
29 Cadwalladr, C. (2016) 'Tech Is Disrupting All before It: Even Democracy Is in Its Sights: The Information Revolution Is Threatening Our Political System' *The Observer* www.theguardian.com/technology/2016/nov/06/technology-disruption-infects-political-system
30 Cadwalladr, C. (2016) 'Google, Democracy and the Truth about Internet Search: Tech-Savvy Rightwingers Have Been Able to "Game" the Algorithms of Internet Giants and Create a New Reality Where Hitler Is a Good Guy, Jews Are Evil and . . . Donald Trump becomes President' *The Observer* www.theguardian.com/technology/2016/dec/04/google-democracy-truth-internet-search-facebook
31 Cadwalladr, C. (2016) 'Google Is Not "Just" a Platform: It Frames, Shapes and Distorts How We See the World' *The Observer* www.theguardian.com/commentisfree/2016/dec/11/google-frames-shapes-and-distorts-how-we-see-world
32 Cadwalladr, C. (2017) 'Follow the Data: Does a Legal Document Link Brexit Campaigns to US Billionaire? We Reveal How a Confidential Legal Agreement Is at the Heart of a Web Connecting Robert Mercer to Britain's EU Referendum' *The Observer* www.theguardian.com/technology/2017/may/14/robert-mercer-cambridge-analytica-leave-eu-referendum-brexit-campaigns
33 Cadwalladr, C. (2017) 'Vote Leave Donations: The Dark Ads, the Mystery "Letter" – and Brexit's Online Guru' *The Guardian* www.theguardian.com/politics/2017/nov/25/vote-leave-dominic-cummings-online-guru-mystery-letter-dark-ads
34 Byrne, J. (2017) 'The Disturbing Reason Why Evangelical Christians Want Jerusalem to Be Israel's Capital' *The Independent* www.indy100.com/article/president-donald-trump-jerusalem-israel-capital-tel-aviv-evangelicals-apocalypse-third-temple-theory-8096596
35 http://wid.world/country/usa/
36 http://wid.world/country/united-kingdom/
37 Jacoby, S.M. (2003) 'Economic Ideas and the Labor Market: Origins of the Anglo-American Model and Prospects for Global Diffusion' *Comparative Labour Law & Policy Journal*, pp. 43–48.
38 Wike, R., Stokes, B., Poushter, J., and Fetterolf, J. (2017) U.S. Image Suffers as Publics Around World Question Trump's Leadership www.pewglobal.org/2017/06/26/tarnished-american-brand/
39 Lis, J. (2017) Brexit's Toll on Foreign Policy: Losing Our Reputation Day after Day www.politics.co.uk/comment-analysis/2017/07/17/brexit-s-toll-on-foreign-policy-losing-our-reputation-day-af
40 Vanbergen, G. (2017) How Brexit Was Engineered by Foreign Billionaires to Bring about Economic Chaos – for Profit http://truepublica.org.uk/contributor-news/how-brexit-was-engineered-by-foreign-billionaires-to-bring-about-economic-chaos-for-profit/
41 Ferziger, J. (2017) Evangelical Christians Head to Jerusalem to Rally Behind Israel. *Bloomberg News* www.bloomberg.com/news/articles/2017-09-19/zionist-evangelicals-trail-trump-to-holy-land-with-cash-in-hand
42 Green, J. (2017) 'How a "Tax Haven" Brexit Threatens the UK's Social Model' *The Conversation* https://theconversation.com/how-a-tax-haven-brexit-threatens-the-uks-social-model-70934

43 Cadwalladr, C. (2016) 'Google, Democracy and the Rruth about Internet Search: Tech-Savvy Rightwingers Have Been Able to "Game" the Algorithms of Internet Giants and Create a New Reality Where Hitler Is a Good Guy, Jews Are Evil and . . . Donald Trump becomes President' *The Observer* www.theguardian.com/technology/2016/dec/04/google-democracy-truth-internet-search-facebook

44 Bilton, N. (2017) '"Oh My God, What Have I Done": Some Early Facebook Employees Regret the Monster They Created' *Vanity Fair* www.vanityfair.com/news/2017/10/early-facebook-employees-regret-the-monster-they-created

45 ibid.

46 Wong, J.C. (2017) 'Former Facebook Executive: Social Media Is Ripping Society Apart' *The Guardian* www.theguardian.com/technology/2017/dec/11/facebook-former-executive-ripping-society-apart

47 ibid.

48 Sulleyman, A. (2017) 'Mark Zuckerberg Asks for Forgiveness and Admits Facebook Has Been Used to "Divide People"' *The Independent* www.independent.co.uk/life-style/gadgets-and-tech/news/facebook-mark-zuckerberg-donald-trump-election-russia-political-ads-fake-news-a7978151.html

49 Hern, A. (2017) Google Plans to "De-Rank" Russia Today and Sputnik to Combat Misinformation www.theguardian.com/technology/2017/nov/21/google-de-rank-russia-today-sputnik-combat-misinformation-alphabet-chief-executive-eric-schmidt

50 Hern, A. (2018) 'Facebook: We Were Too Slow to Recognise Our "Corrosive" Effect on Democracy' *The Guardian* www.theguardian.com/technology/2018/jan/22/facebook-too-slow-social-media-fake-news-hiring

51 McCluhan, M. (1964) *Understanding Media: The Extensions of Man*. Abingdon, Oxon: Routledge Classics, p. 7.

52 Bell, E. (2016) 'Facebook Is Eating the World' *Columbia Journalism Review* www.cjr.org/analysis/facebook_and_media.php

53 Foer, F. (2017) 'Facebook's War on Free Will' *The Guardian* www.theguardian.com/technology/2017/sep/19/facebooks-war-on-free-will

54 ibid.

55 Allen, M. (2017) 'Sean Parker Unloads on Facebook "Exploiting" Human Psychology' *Axios* www.axios.com/sean-parker-unloads-on-facebook-2508036343.html

56 Naughton, J. (2017) 'Why Facebook Is in a Hole over Data Mining' *The Guardian* www.theguardian.com/commentisfree/2017/oct/08/facebook-zuckerberg-in a-hole-data-mining-business-model

57 Kreps, D. (2010) 'My Social Networking Profile: Copy, Resemblance, or Simulacrum? A Poststructuralist Interpretation of Social Information Systems' *European Journal of Information Systems* 19, pp. 104–115.

58 Mantelero, A. (2013) 'The EU Proposal for a General Data Protection Regulation and the Roots of the "Right to Be Forgotten"' *Computer Law & Security Review* 29(3), pp. 229–235.

59 Olivier, J.G.J., Janssens-Maenhout, G., Muntean, M., and Peters, J. *Trends in Global Co2 Emissions 2016 Report*. PBL Netherlands Environmental Assessment Agency, The Hague, The Netherlands http://edgar.jrc.ec.europa.eu/news_docs/jrc-2016-trends-in-global-co2-emissions-2016-report-103425.pdf

60 Klein, N. (2014) *This Changes Everything*. London: Penguin.

61 Schweber, S.S. (1977) 'The Origin of the *Origin* Revisited' *Journal of the History of Biology* 10(2), p. 233.

62 Botkin, D. (1992) *Discordant Harmonies*. Oxford: Oxford University Press, p. 7.

63 ibid., p. 9.

64 ibid.
65 Kauffman, S. (1995) *At Home in the Universe*. Oxford: Oxford University Press, p. 22.
66 Jablonka, E., and Lamb, M.J. (2005) *Evolution in Four Dimensions: Genetic, Epigenetic, Behavioural, and Symbolic Variation in the History of Life*. Cambridge, MA: MIT Press.
67 Oyama, S., Griffiths, P., and Gray, R. (eds.) (2001) *Cycles of Contingency: Developmental Systems and Evolution*. London: MIT Press.
68 Pigliucci, M., and Muller, G. (eds.) (2010) *Evolution: The Extended Synthesis*. London: MIT Press.
69 Gell-Mann, M. (1994) *The Quark and the Jaguar: Adventures in the Simple and the Complex*. London: Abacus, p. 6.
70 Goodwin, B. (1994) *How the Leopard Changed Its Spots*. New York: Charles Scribner & Sons, p. 10.
71 Castellani, B., and Hafferty, F. (2009) *Sociology and Complexity Science*. Berlin: Springer.
72 Kauffman, S. (1995) *At Home in the Universe*. Oxford: Oxford University Press, p. 56.
73 Kauffman, S.A. (1969) 'Metabolic Stability and Epigenesis in Randomly Constructed Genetic Nets' *Journal of Theoretical Biology* 22, pp. 437–467.
74 Kauffman, S.A. (1971) 'Cellular Homeostasis, Epigenesis, and Replication in Randomly Aggregated Macromolecular Systems' *Journal of Cybernetics* 1, pp. 71–96.
75 Goodwin, B. (1994) *How the Leopard Changed Its Spots*. New York: Charles Scribner & Sons, p. 47.
76 ibid.
77 Lorenz, E. (1972) 'Predictability: Does the Flap of a Butterfly's Wing in Brazil Set Off a Tornado in Texas?' *Presentation to the American Association for the Advancement of Science*. Washington, DC.
78 Kauffman, S. (1995) *At Home in the Universe*. Oxford: Oxford University Press, p. 22.
79 Rosen, R. (1978) *Fundamentals of Measurement*. Amsterdam: Elsevier Science, p. 12.
80 Rosen, R. (1985) *Anticipatory Systems*. Oxford: Pergamon Press, p. 424.
81 May, R.M. (1973) *Stability and Complexity in Model Ecosystems*. Princeton, NJ, USA: Princeton University Press.
82 Allen, T.F.H., and Starr, T.B. (1982) *Hierarchy: Perspectives for Ecological Complexity*. Chicago, IL, USA: University of Chicago Press.
83 Maurer, B.A. (1999) *Untangling Ecological Complexity: The Macroscopic Perspective*. Chicago, IL, USA: University of Chicago Press.
84 See www.santafe.edu
85 Jablonka, E., and Lamb, M.J. (2005) *Evolution in Four Dimensions: Genetic, Epigenetic, Behavioural, and Symbolic Variation in the History of Life*. Cambridge, MA: MIT Press.
86 Pigliucci, M., and Muller, G. (eds.) (2010) *Evolution: The Extended Synthesis*. London: MIT Press.
87 Juarrero, A. (2002) *Dynamics in Action: Intentional Behaviour as a Complex System*. London: MIT Press.
88 Thompson, E. (2007) *Mind in Life: Biology, Phenomenology, and the Sciences of Mind*. London: Belknap Harvard.
89 Oyama, S., Griffiths, P., and Gray, R. (eds.) (2001) *Cycles of Contingency: Developmental Systems and Evolution*. London: MIT Press.

90 Crosby, A. (1972) *The Columbian Exchange: Biological and Cultural Consequences of 1492*. Westport, CT: Greenwood Press.
91 Crosby, A. (1986) *Ecological Imperialism: The Biological Expansion of Europe, 900–1900*. Cambridge: Cambridge University Press.
92 Grove, R. (1995/2010) *Green Imperialism: Colonial Expansion, Tropical Island Edens and the Origins of Environmentalism 1600–1860*. Cambridge: Cambridge University Press.
93 Crosby, A. (1986) *Ecological Imperialism: The Biological Expansion of Europe, 900–1900*. Cambridge: Cambridge University Press, p. 31.
94 ibid., p. 38.
95 Ostler, J (2015) Genocide and American Indian History. Oxford Research Encyclopedia of American History. New York: Oxford University Press, p. 3. DOI: 10.1093/acrefore/9780199329175.013.3.
96 Soll, D. (2012) 'Healthy Country, Unhealthy City: Population Growth, Migration, and Urban Sanitation in Lima and Manila' *Global Environment* 5(9), pp. 74–103(30).
97 Crosby, A. (1972) *The Columbian Exchange: Biological and Cultural Consequences of 1492*. Westport, CT: Greenwood Press, p. 64.
98 ibid.
99 ibid., p. 65.
100 ibid.
101 ibid., p. 165.
102 Figures from the US Census Bureau www.census.gov/population/international/data/worldpop/table_history.php
103 Crosby, A. (1972) *The Columbian Exchange: Biological and Cultural Consequences of 1492*. Westport, CT: Greenwood Press, p. 165.
104 McKeown, T. (1976) *The Modern Rise of Population*. London, UK: Edward Arnold.
105 Biraben, J.-N. (1980) 'An Essay Concerning Mankind's Evolution' *Population*, Selected Papers 4, pp. 1–13.
106 Crosby, A. (1972) *The Columbian Exchange: Biological and Cultural Consequences of 1492*. CT: Greenwood Press, p. 170.
107 ibid., p. 170.
108 ibid., p. 175.
109 Crosby, A. (1986) *Ecological Imperialism: The Biological Expansion of Europe, 900–1900*. Cambridge: Cambridge University Press, p. 192.
110 Isenberg, A.C. (2013) 'From the Periphery to the Center: North American Environmental History' *Global Environment* 6(12), p. 87.
111 Cunliffe, B. (2015) *By Steppe, Desert, and Ocean: The Birth of Eurasia*. Oxford: Oxford University Press, p. 37.
112 Cheeseman, T.F. (1906) Manual of the New Zealand Flora. New Zealand: John Mackay, Government Printer, Wellington https://en.wikisource.org/wiki/Manual_of_the_New_Zealand_Flora
113 Wodzicki, J. (1950) 'Introduced Mammals of New Zealand: An Ecological and Economic Survey'. Bulletin 98. Wellington: New Zealand. Dept. of Scientific and Industrial Research.
114 Monbiot, G. (2017) Forget "the Environment": We Need New Words to Convey Life's Wonders www.theguardian.com/commentisfree/2017/aug/09/forget the-environment-new-words-lifes-wonders-language
115 Hallmann, C.A., Sorg, M., Jongejans, E., Siepel, H., Hofland, N., Schwan, H., Stenmans, W., Müller, A., Sumser, H., Hörren, T., Goulson, D., and de Kroon, H.

(2017) 'More Than 75 Percent Decline over 27 Years in Total Flying Insect Biomass in Protected Areas' *PLoS One* https://doi.org/10.1371/journal.pone.0185809, pp. 1–21.

116 Carrington, D. (2017) 'Warning of "Ecological Armageddon" after Dramatic Plunge in Insect Numbers' *The Guardian* www.theguardian.com/environment/2017/oct/18/warning-of-ecological-armageddon-after-dramatic-plunge-in-insect-numbers

117 Monbiot, G. (2017) 'Insectageddon: Farming Is More Catastrophic Than Climate Breakdown' *The Guardian* www.theguardian.com/commentisfree/2017/oct/20/insectageddon-farming-catastrophe-climate-breakdown-insect-populations?CMP=fb_gu

118 Watts, J. (2017) 'Third of Earth's Soil Is Acutely Degraded Due to Agriculture' *The Guardian* www.theguardian.com/environment/2017/sep/12/third-of-earths soil-acutely-degraded-due-to-agriculture-study

119 Bitsch, V. (2000) 'Agricultural Economics and Qualitative Research: Incompatible Paradigms? [16 Paragraphs]' *Forum Qualitative Sozialforschung / Forum: Qualitative Social Research* 1(1), Art. 6 http://nbn-resolving.de/urn:nbn:de:0114-fqs000167

120 Jansen, K. (2009) 'Implicit Sociology, Interdisciplinarity and Systems Theories in Agricultural Science' *Sociologia Ruralis* 49, pp. 172–188 doi: 10.1111/j.1467-9523.2009.00486.x

121 Monbiot, G. (2017) 'Insectageddon: Farming Is More Catastrophic Than Climate Breakdown' *The Guardian* www.theguardian.com/commentisfree/2017/oct/20/insectageddon-farming-catastrophe-climate-breakdown-insect-populations?CMP=fb_gu

122 Myers, S.S., Zanobetti, A., Kloog, I., Huybers, P., Leakey, A.D.B., Bloom, A.J., Carlisle, E., Dietterich, L.H., Fitzgerald, G., Hasegawa, T., Holbrook, N.M., Nelson, R.L., Ottman, M.J., Raboy, V., Sakai, H., Sartor, K.A., Schwartz, J., Seneweera, S., Tausz, M., and Usui, Y. (2014) 'Increasing CO_2 Threatens Human Nutrition' *Nature* 510, pp. 139–142.

123 Loladze, I. (2002) 'Rising CO2 and Human Nutrition: Toward Globally Imbalanced Plant Stoichiometry?' *Trends in Ecology and Evolution* 17, pp. 457–461.

124 Loladze, I. (2014) 'Hidden Shift of the Ionome of Plants Exposed to Elevated CO_2 Depletes Minerals at the Base of Human Nutrition' *eLife* 3, p. e02245.

125 Evich, H.B. (2017) The Great Nutrient Collapse: The Atmosphere Is Literally Changing the Food We Eat, for the Worse: And Almost Nobody Is Paying Attention www.politico.com/agenda/story/2017/09/13/food-nutrients-carbon dioxide-000511

126 Alexandratos, N., and Bruinsma, J. (2012) *World Agriculture towards 2030/2050: The 2012 Revision*. ESA Working Paper No. 12–03. FAO, Rome www.fao.org/docrep/016/ap106e/ap106e.pdf

127 See Alroy, J. (2008) 'Dynamics of Origination and Extinction in the Marine Fossil Record' *Proceedings of the National Academy of Sciences of the United States of America* 105(Supplement 1), pp. 11536–11542.

128 Climate Change (2007) Working Group II: Impacts, Adaptation and Vulnerability 19.3.4 Ecosystems and Biodiversity www.ipcc.ch/publications_and_data/ar4/wg2/en/ch19s19-3-4.html

129 Ceballos, G., Ehrlich, P., Barnosky, A.D., García, A., Pringle, R.M., and Palmer, T.D. (2015) 'Accelerated Modern Human-Induced Species Losses: Entering the Sixth Mass Extinction' *Science Advances* 1(5), p. e1400253.

130 Harvey, F. (2017) 'Nine of World's Biggest Fishing Firms Sign Up to Protect Oceans' *The Guardian* www.theguardian.com/environment/2017/jun/09/nine-of-worlds-biggest-fishing-firms-sign-up-to-protect-oceans
131 Cheng, L., Trenberth, K.E., Fasullo, J., Boyer, T., Abraham, J., and Zhu, J. (2017) 'Improved Estimates of Ocean Heat Content from 1960 to 2015' *Science Advances* 3(3), p. e1601545.
132 Johnson, D. (2017) 'Is This the Worst Hurricane Season Ever? Here's How It Compares' *Time Magazine* http://time.com/4952628/hurricane-season-harvey irma-jose-maria/
133 Fujita, R. (2017) 5 Ways Climate Change Is Affecting Our Oceans www.edf.org/blog/2013/10/08/5-ways-climate-change-affecting-our-oceans
134 ibid.
135 Carrington, D. (2017) 'Plastic Fibres Found in Tap Water Around the World, Study Reveals' *The Guardian* www.theguardian.com/environment/2017/sep/06/plastic-fibres-found-tap-water-around-world-study-reveals
136 Tyree, C., and Morrison, D. (2017) Invisibles: The Plastic Inside Us https://orbmedia.org/stories/Invisibles_plastics
137 Embury-Dennis, T. (2017) 'Tide of Plastic Rubbish Discovered Floating Off Idyllic Caribbean Island Coastline' *The Independent* www.independent.co.uk/news/world/americas/plastic-rubbish-tide-caribbean-island-roatan-honduras-coast-pollution-a8017381.html
138 Sharma, S., and Chatterjee, S. (2017) 'Microplastic Pollution, a Threat to Marine Ecosystem and Human Health: A Short Review' *Environmental Science and Pollution Research* 24(27), pp. 21530–21547.
139 Floridi, L. (2014) 'Open Data, Data Protection, and Group Privacy' *Philosophy of Technology* 27, pp. 1–3.
140 Springmann, M., Godfraya, H.C.J., Raynera, M., and Scarborough, P. (2016) 'Analysis and Valuation of the Health and Climate Change Cobenefits of Dietary Change' *PNAS* 113(15) www.pnas.org/content/113/15/4146.abstract

5 A theoretical manifesto for Green IT

Process-relational social organisation

As we saw in Chapter 3 through the eyes of Bergson and Whitehead, all matter and subjectivity are interrelated in an ongoing processual flow, rather than the universe being merely discrete and discontinuous things with no subjectivity at all. As we saw in Chapter 4, this means that a number of choices are in fact clearer for us than might otherwise appear, showing us that interpretivism is closer to reality than positivism in IS, collectivism is a necessary balance to individualism, and complexity is a far more accurate scientific picture of the universe than reductionism can bring us. It makes sense, then, when we come to consider how we organise our societies that we recognise that we are not islands and that much must be 'held in common.' We are individuals, of course, but we cannot survive alone, and what we gain from living within a social grouping we are thus bound to return to in kind. Appealing only to our individual interests, to justify any social contract, moreover, reduces us to beings only interested in ourselves, and this is a distorting picture. There are, in short, both rights and responsibilities, and other reasons besides, for living together. We cannot live alone, and we must take part in collective efforts for the good of all, and not just because it is in our own interest. Methodological individualism must be replaced at the core of our thinking, inspired by the understandings gained from process-relational philosophy, from complexity theory, and from moral philosophy that show us that a society is far more than an aggregate of individuals, that the whole is indeed greater than the sum of its component parts, especially when dealing with *systems*, whether those systems are social systems, ecosystems, or information systems. In brief, the libertarian argument for the neoliberal capitalist society runs counter not only to the morality of egalitarianism, but to the reality of the natural world of which we are a part.

Nozick: the Wilt Chamberlain example

First, methodological individualism in philosophy must be eschewed. Nozick bases one of his most famous libertarian arguments for the rights of self-owning individuals to be free of the 'tyranny and injustice' of any responsibility to society upon the example of a basketball player. Imagine, for a moment, a situation which – after Nozick – we shall label D1, in which a society 'upholds some principle of equality in the distribution of benefits enjoyed and burdens borne by its members.'[1] Nozick is opposed to *any* such principle. Here is Nozick, describing this example, from *Anarchy, State and Utopia:*

> [S]uppose that Wilt Chamberlain is greatly in demand by basketball teams, being a great gate attraction . . . He signs the following sort of contract with a team: In each home game, twenty-five cents from the price of each ticket of admission goes to him . . . The season starts, and people cheerfully attend his team's games; they buy their tickets, each time dropping separate twenty-five cents of their admission price into a special box with Chamberlain's name on it. They are excited about seeing him play; it is worth the total admission price to them. Let us suppose that in one season 1 million persons attend his home games, and Wilt Chamberlain winds up with $250,000, a much larger sum than the average income. . . . Is he entitled to this income? Is this new distribution, D2, unjust? If so, why? . . . If D1 was a just distribution, and people voluntarily moved from it to D2, transferring parts of their shares they were given under D1 (what was it for if not to do something with?), isn't D2 also just? If people were entitled to dispose of the resources to which they were entitled (under D1), didn't this include their being entitled to give it to, or exchange it with, Wilt Chamberlain?[2]

For Nozick, disturbingly, the situation in which Wilt Chamberlain would find himself if the state then decided to take away, in the form of taxation, any of this share which people had given to him would constitute a tyranny that enslaved him and should be condemned as such. Nozick uses this example to argue for inalienable rights *not* to be treated as a slave and condemns nearly all forms of taxation as forces of enslavement. Needless to say, many have countered these extreme views.

Murphy and Nagel: a liberal answer to Nozick

For Murphy and Nagel, the entire notion of private property is, in the first place, 'a legal convention, defined in part by the tax system.'[3] Take the example of how William the Conqueror changed the system in England in the 11th century. Previously the Anglo-Saxon thegns provided the sovereign with arms and soldiers as a tax upon their landholdings. Under William, the estates within the kingdom he now *owned* belonged only to the king's cousins and generals *at his discretion*, for the purpose of raising taxes for, and fighting for, the Crown: fail to turn up, and they lost their land. A tax system, therefore, 'cannot be evaluated by looking at its impact on private property'[4] because the overall system of property rights is in part created by taxation. 'Justice or injustice in taxation can only mean justice or injustice in the system of property rights and entitlements that result from a particular tax regime.'[5] Our contemporary tax regime, in the United States and UK at least, where the wealthier you are the less likely it is that you will pay any tax at all,[6] stems from the kind of Nozickian antipathy described earlier and conjures a picture of rather medieval robber barons – like the later Normans who fought weaker successors to William.

It is important for Murphy and Nagel when considering taxation to distinguish between redistribution and public provision. These are two different approaches to the spending of the money gathered by governments in the form of tax, and one can argue in favour of one over the other, or for any range of mixing of the two. Most countries undertake some blend of both (i) redistribution, in the form of money transfers and of cash subsidies to combat poverty and to support people in retirement, and (ii) public provision, in the form of 'public education, health care, military expenditure, environmental and social control, support for science, art, sport, entertainment, and culture.'[7] Having made this distinction, it becomes clear that how the initial settlement for distribution is settled – whether upon egalitarian, utilitarian, or liberal principles – is the principal matter of debate with respect to Nozick's libertarianism, and not how the money is then spent.

Liberty is the key concept in political theory, most familiar in the elements of the social contract by which the power of the state over individuals is limited. Key rights of liberty such as 'freedom of expression, freedom of religion, freedom of association, privacy, and the protection of the person against physical violation'[8] are standard in 'liberal' societies. For property-owning democracies, we add to these rights 'economic freedom' – the freedom to 'hold personal property with discretion to do what one wants with it.'[9] Now Nozick's extreme position is that the only justification for any interference in one's *economic* freedom 'would be the protection of those [aforementioned] and other comparably important rights themselves.'[10] Economic freedom thereby becomes the most important of all the freedoms. In this case, only the most limited forms of public provision – the military, the police, the judiciary – can be justified, and taxation thereby restricted wholly to such specific public provision, with no redistribution of any kind, and nothing to promote general welfare in the form of health, science, art, etc. Some anarcho-libertarians (e.g. Murray Rothbard)[11] even promote the idea of private police forces over any public provision at all. Such a principled objection to almost any restrictions upon economic freedom – whether at this Nozickian extreme or at some lesser point near to it – are what underlie the political opposition to taxation in some Anglo-American political circles and have encouraged the expansion of the use of the tax havens.[12]

More egalitarian liberals, by contrast, see absolutely 'no moral similarity between the right to speak one's mind, to practice one's religion, or to act on one's sexual inclinations, and the right to enter into a labour contract or a sale of property unencumbered by a tax bite.'[13]

Cohen: a Marxist answer to Nozick

For Cohen – one of Nozick's main critics – from the Marxist perspective, there are any number of finer arguments, principally concerning the backdrop of the example, against Nozick's Wilt Chamberlain story. The fact, for instance, that Nozick's redistributing D1 pre-exists the new D2 (in the example, but not in the real world) and that concepts of 'just deserts' more proper to D2 being the pre-existing state of affairs are appealed to render the story incoherent for Cohen. But the central issue in my reading of Cohen's treatment of this example is that

> among the reasons for limiting how much an individual may hold, regardless of how he came to hold it, is to prevent him from acquiring, through his holdings, an unacceptable amount of power over others: the Chamberlain transaction looks less harmless when we focus on that consideration.[14]

In Cohen's socialist society – a properly egalitarian D1 – the transaction would be unlikely to be entered into so voluntarily in any case, because people would 'refrain from so contracting as to upset the equality they prize,'[15] especially as such a transfer of wealth would likely have generational impacts.

Taxation, therefore, in some form of redistributive and public-provision settlement, should be there to ensure not only that no one gains such wealth as to concentrate power over others into their own hands, but to ensure that such wealth and power is not inherited, either. The notion that such taxation renders those such as Wilt Chamberlain 'slaves' of those who benefit from state spending requires an extraordinary double-think around the notion of a 'slave state.' Slavery in contemporary capitalist societies is illegal – it is a civil right not to be enslaved – though the more neoliberal a society becomes, the less is spent on policing such a right, and the more 'modern-day' slavery is prevalent.[16]

One has the *right*, in other words, in such societies to work for no one. One of Cohen's arguments against libertarian capitalism, however, is that only a tiny number of those living in a capitalist society may have the *power* to work for no one. The rest 'are *forced* to work for some or other person or group. Their natural rights are not matched by corresponding effective powers.'[17] Thus, Cohen concludes that, in effect, contrary to avoiding any 'enslavement' of the Wilt Chamberlains of this world, '"libertarian" capitalism sacrifices liberty to capitalism'[18] and effectively enslaves the rest of us.

A moral answer to Nozick

The most insightful critique of individualism, however, to my mind, comes not from the liberal or socialist counter-arguments presented earlier, but from a moral political science. Whilst gladly recognising the usefulness of the notion of 'rational choice' in social modelling and political theory more widely, the moral complaint is that the 'claim that self-interest alone motivates political behaviour must be either vacuous, if self-interest can encompass any motive, or false, if self-interest means behaviour that consciously intends only the self as the beneficiary.'[19] Context is key. Specifying contexts in which narrowly self-interested behaviour is most likely, and least likely, to appear enables modellers of political behaviour to suggest normative contexts – where outcomes and motives that are good in themselves are promoted – whilst discouraging others. Rational economic 'man,' after all – especially the one whose economic freedom is paramount above all else – is only such while 'he' is consistent. A theory in which choosing x over y reveals your preferences is completely agnostic about whether those preferences reveal you are 'a single-minded egoist or a raving altruist or a class-conscious militant, you will appear to be maximising your own utility'[20] if you remain consistent. Rational choice theory, for Amartya Sen, in other words, involves nothing other than internal consistency, and as Mansbridge affirms, without *context*, policy based upon this is apt to generate less-than-savoury outcomes.

The assumption of self-interest, given originally by Thomas Hobbes, is a picture of man in the 'state of nature' embedded in original sin. Hobbes was writing at a time when Christianity held a foundational sway over the lives and minds of Europeans. For all that Hobbes tried to create a materialist understanding of human nature, his notion that without the constraint of sovereign power life would be 'nasty, brutish and short' and that this 'state of nature' would be a war of all against all remained in the grip of a view of humanity that we are all born sinners. Hobbes, according to later critics such as Bayle and d'Holbach, was prone to a 'fear of phantoms and demons'[21] and acknowledged in his writings the likely existence of miracles.[22] To ascribe his low opinion of humanity to a cultural immersion in the notion of 'original sin' is not inconsistent with his reputation as one of the early 'atheists,' but to acknowledge the context in which he wrote and the *episteme*[23] in which his ideas necessarily sat. That this view of humanity is embedded in Western political theory is evident in the economic theories that place calculations of self-interest – otherwise known as selfishness – at the core of all human activity.

Altruism can – and does – sit alongside self-interest in the heart of human activity. As Goodwin underlines when discussing the evolution of the human species, we are indeed every bit 'as altruistic as we are selfish.'[24] To say that love, for example, can be reduced to self-interest alone, as if a gift were only for the glow of self-satisfaction another's pleasure might bring one, is as absurd as to suggest that all motivations could be reduced to altruism. (How could anyone's pleasure be satisfied by another's generosity, if only generosity lay at the root?) Now 'if some are to be altruistic,' one might argue, 'others must be selfish, at least some of the time, but everybody *could* be selfish all the time.'[25] Granted, but this is again that reductionist desire to seek out the mathematical precision of simplicity, when the truer answer is likely far more complex. William of Ockham, the 14th-century English philosopher who first suggested the principle that entities should not be multiplied beyond what is necessary – Ockham's famous 'razor' – did not thereby suggest that all things must instead be reduced to a simplicity that occurs only in the most unnatural conditions. Understanding reality requires addressing the real, not creating false conditions in which things seem simpler and more manageable – Whitehead's Fallacy of Misplaced Concreteness once more. Whilst for pragmatic purposes this kind of approach may indeed prove useful on occasion, it nonetheless flies in the face of the very evident multiplicity and continual difference we find in the world around us: the very absence of such simplicity. In the real world, indeed,

> some forms of helping behaviour are not reciprocated and so cannot be explained by long-term self-interest. Parents have a selfish interest in helping their children, assuming that children will care for parents in their old age – but it is not in the selfish interest of children to provide for such care.[26]

Yet many still do.

Everybody *could* be selfish all the time, but – unless social policy deliberately nudges us all in that direction – in the right context people willingly and happily are *not* selfish all of the time. Anonymous contributions to impersonal charities – blood donation, no less – are a case in point. There is no social opprobrium to be avoided by doing so, and no gain of social standing to be acquired by doing so. There are, indeed, any number of social science approaches to this – concepts like 'socialisation,' 'operant conditioning,' and 'deterrence' – trying to 'nudge' citizens towards unselfishness. What many have found, of course, is that Hobbes' ideas are missing a fundamental and profound element: we have moral ideas and try to do what is right. Empathy – our ability to experience pain and pleasure ourselves, and therefore to imagine it in others – stands in the way of pure selfishness. The 'viability of the social contract depends not just on society's capacity to inspire fear in the hearts of potential violators' – Hobbes' sovereign might – 'but on its capacity to develop the empathic tendencies from which moral sentiments derive.'[27]

A process-relational answer to Nozick

The process-relational answer to Nozick's individualism is already quite clear: even islands are connected if you but look beneath the waves. Bergson's political philosophy lay mostly in his activities as a public figure rather than in his writings. His main 'political contribution was his work with the Wilson administration to establish the League of Nations.'[28] The League was an intergovernmental organisation founded in 1920 in the aftermath of war, whose principal mission was to maintain world peace, and it comprised almost 60 member countries by the mid-1930s. (It foundered when the Axis powers left and the world descended once again into war, but was replaced in 1946 by the United Nations.) His work with the League of Nations reached its pinnacle shortly after his retirement from academia, when he was appointed, in 1922, first president of the League's International Commission on Intellectual Cooperation (ICIC), an attempt to show that intellectuals could work together at an international level, which included Einstein, Marie Curie, and many others. After the Second World War, this work flowered into one of the finest global organisations of all, the replacement for the ICIC: the United Nations Educational, Scientific and Cultural Organization, commonly known simply as UNESCO.

In his writings, Bergson stressed the importance of openness versus closure in international relations. In *Two Sources of Morality and Religion*, in the first part, Bergson defined humanity in relation to a characteristic deconstruction of opposites: between the notion of societies and of society; between that which is closed and that which is open. Bergson offered a description of the social as a system of obligation. A great believer in free choice, a faculty which consciousness grants us, Bergson was all too aware that choice is soon overlaid by the necessary coordination required of social grouping.

> While his consciousness, delving downwards, reveals to him, the deeper he goes, an ever more original personality, incommensurable with the others and indeed undefinable in words, on the surface of life we are in continuous contact with other men whom we resemble, and united to them by a discipline which creates between them and us a relation of interdependence.[29]

This discipline and interdependence comprise a foundational moral obligation to one another that forms the glue of social grouping. But these groupings are always, by definition, ultimately closed. Any individual grouping, be it family, clan, tribe, academic discipline, nation, or even a grouping of nations such as Europe, or 'the West,' is 'to include at any moment a certain number of individuals, and exclude others.'[30] For Bergson this is a 'natural' state, akin to the societies created by that other most social of earth's creatures, the ant. Yet this is no simple biodeterminism, for Bergson is clear on the essential point that human consciousness not only marks a fundamental distinction between us and the ant, but that consciousness itself is of a radically different nature from anything that science has yet approached – in part because it lies on the other side of a divide at the foundation of modern science itself. Having carved out his belief in human choice at the beginning of his career in *Time and Free Will*, in his last book, *The Two Sources of Morality and Religion*, it is in the distinction between the closed and the open that Bergson finds choice at its most powerful, and its most human. 'Between the society in which we live and humanity in general there is . . . the same contrast as between the closed and the open; the difference between the two objects is one of kind and not simply one of degree.'[31] The spirit of the League of Nations and the ICIC, still alive in the United Nations and UNESCO, is imbued with just this very openness, an expansive inclusivity very different from the closed exclusivity of nationalism.

Whitehead did not directly address political philosophy in his work, but 'did produce a considerable volume of material concerning social and political issues.'[32] In life, in the UK, he was a Liberal reformer supporting the liberal wing of the Labour Party and a strong supporter of the Women's Suffrage movement (and was chair, no less, in 1907, of the Cambridge branch of the Men's League for Women's Suffrage).[33] In his writings, Whitehead frequently makes a critique of individualism, as one would expect. Importantly, he does not deny the existence – and indeed centrality, in political theory – of the individual whilst at the same time underscoring how no individual can exist alone. He argues that the idea of the self-sufficient individual only externally related to others through a contract, and the doctrine of competitive and possessive individualism that goes with it, are among the abstractions he contends we all too often reify, much to our detriment. Nor, however, does Whitehead support the more Soviet model that would err in the opposite direction. As Rice puts it, Whitehead's approach 'serves as a ground for rejecting both any ideology calling for the sacrifice of concrete individuals in the name of some reified notion of society or the state, and any ideology resting on an abstract conception of the individual.'[34] In similar fashion to Bergson's uniqueness at the root, to which the downward delving consciousness strives, Whitehead finds that it is in the interior, subjective self-enjoyment that an Actual Occasion sits absolutely individuated and apart from all other Actual Occasions, whilst, on the surface of life, it is merely another part of the universal interrelatedness and ongoing flow of existence.

This balance, for both Bergson and Whitehead, between the irreducibly individual internal subjectivity of self and the inescapable interconnectedness of the processual flow of existence led each of them to support in the early 20th century reforming and left-leaning political movements that eschewed both the possessive individualism of the capitalist right and the homogenising social structures of the far Soviet left of the time.

What Bergson or Whitehead would have made of the ecological dangers of our era can only be guessed at. As Poisson points out, however, 'The lack of connectedness of economic activity to the biophysical environment in neoclassical economic theory is a problem that did not go unnoticed by Whitehead.'[35]

Ecological economics

What has been becoming clear for many critics of today's neoliberalism is that the focus upon economic freedom amongst the libertarians has distorted neoclassical economics into an obsession with 'more markets, less government' as the answer to all economic questions. This is clearly just a part of their mission to pay no tax, and paying no tax is something which no neoclassical economists themselves ever signed up for. 'Good economists know that the correct answer to any question in economics is: it depends,'[36] as one journalist put it recently. Private property rights and the tax systems that define them are a necessary part of any capitalist economy, and a broad tax base is one thing neoclassical economics in fact recommends.

For critics of individualism, all this is a case of life imitating art. Much economics has become a distortion of the human – making us fit as neatly as possible into mathematical models, rather than attempting to model our behaviour. From Adam Smith onward, economics has sought to mathematicise – and render more and more positivist – its understanding of the financial workings of society to the point where governments began to attempt to 'nudge'[37] us all into being a more and more perfect fit for the models they came to believe are best. A 'good citizen' today is a 'good consumer,' chasing after her or his own self-interest, making rational calculations concerning how best she or he can ensure competitive margin over her or his fellows. We are trying to eradicate – or at least ignore – altruism in the pursuit of a more efficient economy. *Homo economicus* – the 'solitary figure poised with money in his hand, calculator in his head, nature at his feet, and an insatiable appetite in his heart,'[38] is a picture of Man the Individual, with a 200-year-old pedigree, drawn gradually ever more closely and precisely, excluding along the way all that made it more difficult to fit him into mathematical models.

As we learned from Hermann E. Daly as long ago as 1973, however, what was really most wrong with 19th-century classical economics was the misery of the working class, 'misery which gave the lie to the belief that [Adam Smith's] invisible hand could effectively prevent exploitation.'[39] Marx tried to shift the focus from competition within each class to the competition *between* the classes, which he believed would lead inevitably to revolution. Capitalism proved extremely good at self-reinvention, however, especially through global conflict. Neoclassical economists shifted the focus back again to the atomism of Adam Smith, acknowledging a notion of imperfect competition as they did so. But the real innovation of neoclassical economics was to reconceive of 'net value' as the result of 'psychic want satisfaction' rather than the 'product of labour.'

> The origin of the value was subjective, not objective. The focus was not on distribution among classes but on the efficiency of allocation – how could a society get the maximum amount of want satisfaction from scarce resources, *given* a certain distribution of wealth and income among individuals and social classes. Pure competition [. . .] provided the optimal allocation.[40]

Shocked by the poverty of the 1930s, Keynes tried to shift the focus again towards full employment 'and optimal microeconomic allocation of resources.' But now, '[t]he *summum bonum* to be maximised is no longer psychic want satisfaction, which is unmeasurable, but annual aggregate real output, GNP – Gross National Product – a value index of the quantity flow of annual production.'[41] This Keynesian-neoclassical combination, then, promoted continual growth. The neoliberal, or 'Washington,' consensus that displaced it by the end of the 1970s, worse still, promoted continual growth without any fear of unemployment or poverty!

But, as Daly pointed out, 'in a finite world continual growth is impossible. Given finite stomachs, finite lifetimes, and the kind of man who does not live by bread alone, growth becomes undesirable long before it becomes impossible.'[42] The assumption, however, that 'aggregate wants are infinite and should be served by trying to make aggregate production infinite, and that technology is an omnipotent *deus ex machina* who (sic) will get us out of any growth-induced problems'[43] continues to guide economists and politicians to this day. Today's financialised economies have become completely divorced from any appreciation of Daly's ultimate and fundamental point: 'nature really does impose "an inescapable general scarcity," and it is a serious delusion to believe otherwise.'[44]

There are limits, in other words, to growth, and 'sustainability' must govern our economic thinking. The UN-sponsored 1987 Brundtland Commission report, *Our Common Future*,[45] defined sustainable development as being to meet 'the needs of the present without compromising the ability of future generations to meet their own needs.' Such a definition seemed, for many years, rather vague,[46] but the 17 Sustainable Development Goals of 2015, with their 169 individual targets,[47] made the definition all the more precise. To properly achieve any of this, however, a huge rethinking of economics is needed.

Fortunately, this rethinking seems to be underway – and led by students. The '33 Theses for an Economics Reformation' posted in December 2017 to the doors of the London School of Economics in a nod to Martin Luther's apocryphal Protestant Reformation theses in Wittenberg, five centuries ago, represents a groundswell of opinion challenging the 'intellectual monopoly' around the 'neoclassical perspective' that has developed in the discipline of economics, to the exclusion of healthy debate, and accuses this monopoly of becoming more of a faith than a science.[48] There is solid work, too, going into the redemption of the state, for example, in economist William Mitchell and political theorist Thomas Fazi's *Reclaiming the State: A Progressive Vision of Sovereignty for a Post-Neoliberal World*,[49] and in the proposals for reversing the programme of privatisation undertaken over the last several decades.[50] The belief that common ownership of a resource causes its demise, prompted by biologist Garrett Hardin's flawed 1968 paper published in *Science*, famously entitled, 'The Tragedy of the Commons,' is being newly challenged and debunked.[51] As Locher describes it, such a 'tragedy' was 'a misconception with no concrete basis, skewed by a highly ideological perception of social systems.'[52]

Let us not forget, Jevons, Walras, and the other founding neoclassical economists concocted their analytical, scientific, economic theory in the heat of the 'socialist calculation controversy' of the 1930s as a means to prove that no form of state interference in economics was either necessary or desirable – in contrast to the state socialist model of central planning economics being attempted in the Soviet world.[53] Each side believed their own version was the 'rational, scientific' way to run an economy. The later neoliberal fixation upon economic freedom – and thus against taxation – was thus pushing against an open door in its distaste for the state. But both these sets of ideas have run their course. The crisis of 2007–2008 was the fatal blow to neoclassical economics' credibility, and the decade since merely the death throes of the spent ideology of neoliberalism. The right-wing ideologues – cartoon baddies in a social media age – and the smell of Russian espionage[54] and billionaire manipulation[55,56] behind them, reveal little more than greed at the helm of a movement without intellectual foundation.

Kate Raworth – one of the economists who promoted the '33 Theses' on their publication – draws a marvellous contrast between what these neoclassical economists created and what, in the 21st century, it is clear we increasingly need (Table 5.1).

This neoclassical picture was not implemented in the 1930s, of course. In fact, Soviet-style central planning – precisely what it was created to oppose – was what was immediately applied across the UK and United States by the likes of Vannavar Bush and Warren Weaver[57] and came to be known as the military-industrial complex: the complete government-organised control of the economy for total war. In the late 1940s, once Fascism had been defeated, much of that complex was not immediately deconstructed as the Cold War ensued. It took the philosophy of Robert Nozick, no less, and the New Right neoliberal philosophy of the mid-to-late 1970s, to finally bring this neoclassical economic agenda to the fore and into the seats of government. Thatcher and Reagan – among others – armed with Hayek's and Friedman's economics and Nozick's individualism, brought us the neoliberal world, finally, in the 1980s. It took, then, until the financial crisis of 2007–2008, for the world to realise actually what folly neoliberalism – just like its old adversary Soviet central planning – turned out to be.

Table 5.1 20th-century neoclassical economics

	20th-century neoclassical economics
THE MARKET	*Which is efficient – so give it free rein*
BUSINESS	*Which is innovative – so let it lead*
FINANCE	*Which is infallible – so trust in its ways*
TRADE	*Which is win-win – so open your borders*
THE STATE	*Which is incompetent – so don't let it meddle*
Plus other characters not required on stage	
THE HOUSEHOLD	*Which is domestic – so leave it to the women*
THE COMMONS	*Which are tragic – so sell them off*
SOCIETY	*Which is non-existent – so ignore it*
EARTH	*Which is inexhaustible – so take all you want*
POWER	*Which is irrelevant – so don't mention it*

Source: Raworth, Kate (2017) *Doughnut Economics* Milton Keynes: Penguin Random House pp. 68–70

Kate Raworth's new alternative economics speaks more nearly to common sense than to the positivist fixation with mathematical rationality. She sees the market, most importantly, as embedded within a wider economy, including the household, the earth, and society at large, rather than some self-contained – and thus easily calculable – entity. Human beings populate Raworth's economy, moreover, not 'rational economic man.' The network dynamics of complex systems[58] are interrogated and taken account of, rather than the stale mechanical equilibrium models of the 19th century. Redistribution is designed into Raworth's economic model, rather than trusting to permanent economic growth to lift people out of relative poverty. Her 'doughnut' design for the economy regenerates and restores, rather than depletes and wastes. Table 5.2 shows how the elements of 'doughnut' economics work together.[59]

Outside of the old economic models and the social policies that try to make us fit into them, the real world continues to be, thankfully, a much richer and more complex place. Even Adam Smith, we are finding out more recently from careful historical reconstruction,[60] had a mother who kept house and made meals for him, day in, day out. Adam never married and lived at home as he wrote, never mentioning the crucial part of the economy that kept food upon his table, the labour – and the love – that provided comfort, warmth, and a home where he could put his feet up at the end of the day. The household, in short, a core contribution to any society's economy, is completely omitted from the (neo)classical economic plan – just as it is overlooked in the neoliberal political philosophy whose self-interested individuals are always men. The household, in these 'rational' models, is simply left to the women.

Table 5.2 21st-century economics

	21st-century 'doughnut' economics
EARTH	*Which is life-giving – so respect its boundaries*
SOCIETY	*Which is foundational – so nurture its connections*
THE ECONOMY	*Which is diverse – so support all its systems*
THE MARKET	*Which is powerful – so embed it wisely*
THE COMMONS	*Which are creative – so unleash their potential*
THE STATE	*Which is essential – so make it accountable*
FINANCE	*Which is in service – so make it serve society*
BUSINESS	*Which is innovative – so give it purpose*
TRADE	*Which is double-edged – so make it fair*
POWER	*Which is pervasive – so check its abuse*

Source: Raworth, Kate (2017) *Doughnut Economics* Milton Keynes: Penguin Random House p. 72

Ecological care and reality

The '33 Theses' and the growing groundswell – or 'youthquake[61]' – amongst young people in the UK and United States show that there is still hope, if, indeed, still a long way to go. Legal moves are underway to challenge the polluters and protect the environment[62] and to reclaim the billions of dollars accumulated by the creators of climate change and to fund measures to counter its worst effects. Ground-breaking research by the Climate Accountability Institute in 2014 brought us a quantitative analysis of historic emissions that has traced 'sources of industrial CO_2 and methane to the 90 largest corporate investor-owned and state-owned producers of fossil fuels and cement from as early as 1854 to 2010.'[63] This research – recently updated[64] – now lists 100 fossil fuel producers and nearly 1 trillion tonnes of greenhouse gas emissions, revealing that a mere '50 corporations account for more than one-fifth of all carbon released into the atmosphere since the industrial revolution began.'[65] Many of these corporations are now subject to legal proceedings in Australia[66] and in the United States, where the city attorneys of San Francisco, Oakland, and New York are taking BP, Royal Dutch Shell, Exxon Mobil, Chevron, and ConocoPhillips to court.[67,68,69]

Instead of fossil capitalism, it turns out that – according to a study by multinational finance and asset management consultancy, Lazard[70] – renewable energy sources are in fact cheaper. But it is also becoming clear that the individualism of the neoliberal agenda is proving an obstacle in the shift away from fossil capitalism. In a neoliberal world, the onus is upon the individual to do their own personal recycling, make their own economic choices regarding 'greener' products, and so forth. In other words, we should rely upon the market to shift our economies toward sustainability. But such micro-efforts are not working, because they are not sufficient. Such personal environmental behaviour, according to one recent study, makes little impact on overall carbon emissions.[71] If affordable public transport isn't available, people will commute with cars. If local organic food is too expensive, people will continue to shop at fossil fuel–intensive supermarkets. Neoliberalism attempts to persuade us to address climate change through our wallets, rather than through power and politics, *because* such a strategy underlines their individualist agenda. Large-scale – and urgent – government-led action, in the form of regulations that curb emissions, divestment that starves polluters of investment,[72] and the switching of subsidies for fossil fuels[73] to renewable energy sources is what is needed. The 'market' will not make this happen, but social and political movements favouring a stronger role for the state just might.

There is also hope that some of the worst ecological problems we face may yet be fixed. The vast quantities of waste plastic polluting the environment[74] may not be quite as seemingly permanent a problem as feared. As well as any number of innovative waste collection mechanisms for gathering the debris on the surface of the oceans, a bacterium that eats plastic, which evolved naturally in a Japanese waste-dump, has been tweaked in a UK laboratory and holds much promise.[75] Concerted efforts are beginning to stop plastic getting into the oceans[76] and – more importantly – to reduce the amount we make and use in the first place. The petrochemical industry producing the myriad products upon which our societies depend that do not, in themselves, contribute to carbon emissions needs to focus upon the principles of the 'circular economy'[77] being encouraged in the EU, ensuring that what hydrocarbons are left for us to dig up are used not for burning, nor for the kinds of plastics that last for 10,000 years, but in innovative products with a recyclable end-life, that contribute positively to our societies.

The effects of climate change already created will have to be dealt with anyway. It's too late to stop a lot of the damage already done and the changes that are now unavoidable. There's hope we can stop it from getting a lot worse, but there are impacts we'll have to deal with now that are too late to avoid. This means we need to change our politics. To change our politics, we need to understand the philosophy behind it and change how we think about ourselves and about the world. This book is an attempt to address how we should think about the digital in this context.

Infomateriality

The community of scholars in the field of Information Systems needs to change its understanding of what the role of the digital *ought* to be in a world newly understood from the shift in philosophical standpoint outlined in this book.

Hirschheim and Klein point out in their history of Information Systems that there have been many unsuccessful attempts to define IS. My suggestion, in this book, has been that French philosopher Henri Bergson and British mathematician and philosopher Alfred North Whitehead's process philosophy offers an ontological grounding through which we might newly understand the field – first of all by seriously broadening our horizons. Much of the material covered in this book – philosophy, ecology, economics, politics, critical theory – is rarely to be found in academic work on information systems, at least overtly. It should be clear by now, however, to the reader, that *a* philosophy and *a* politics and *an* economics nonetheless underpin everything that is done in information systems and that our impact upon the ecology of our world is a direct result of this implicit, unstated, undiscussed set of foundational ideas.

Much of information systems as a field, and its practical applications in the digital world, it is clear, is in service to the agenda of neoliberalism's most pernicious versions of neoclassical economics and, as such, contributes to the destruction of the environment. It contributes to the impoverishment of our sense of ourselves as citizens, rather than merely consumers, to the marginalising of the altruism that sits alongside the self-interest in the complex ways in which we relate to one another, depend on one another, and contribute to the wider society of which we are a part.

Ultimately, the implications of our foray in Chapter 3 into the ontological metaphysics of Bergson and Whitehead, for our understanding of the nature of information systems, cuts right through Chua's classification of research epistemologies into positivist, interpretive, and critical,[78] suggesting that in fact these streams are approaches to something unitary that, through the application of filters, attempt to screen out aspects of reality that do not fit well into the researcher's approach. In a rough and undernuanced sketch, one might caricature the three approaches in the following manner: the positivist researcher approaches information systems screening out the reality of subjective consciousness and pretending that the 'rational agent user' is an apolitical and atheoretical depiction of the human condition, rather than a specific tool of neoclassical economic theory and neoliberal politics.

The interpretivist researcher situates herself on the side of the ontological dilemma in sociology with those who demarcate social reality from physical existence, screening out the parameters of practical constraints. The critical researcher, in turn, screens out the positivist origins of IS history, pretending that a science built on mathematical logic funded by defence budgets and corporations can easily be bent toward effecting social good. Again, these are caricatures, and the reality is inevitably more nuanced, but the cartoon carries a message: something about the nature of IS. As Hirschheim and Klein suggested when discussing the use of social theorists like Giddens, Latour, and Habermas to illumine IS phenomena, I would further characterise the three main streams of IS research as being 'like different telescopes focusing on different objects, with each telescope associated with its own set of research methods.'[79]

What, then, in the end, *is* an information system? We are all used to speaking of the computer hardware at one end and the people at the other end of a spectrum of influences, stakeholders, components, relations. Positivists deal with one end, interpretivists with the other. But the physical bodies of the people, the fingers touching the keyboard, and the eyes scanning the screens are as much 'hardware' as the cabling, circuit boards, and haptic interfaces: to the bioinformaticians and bioengineers the human hardware is increasingly becoming blurred with the silicon, not just through the still-simmering phenomenon of 'wetware,'[80] but through the very thriving phenomenon of the quantified self,[81] through which our physical health and fitness are monitored, tracked, organised, and driven in a sea of data. Similarly, the social practices, power relations, and embedded politics within the artefacts of our computing hardware define all such *technē*[82] as fundamentally social, as opposed to natural, as much a set of simple 'material things' as a field system imposed upon the once-wild ecology of a valley. An information system, therefore, is something not only exemplary of, but defined by – perhaps only properly understandable in the context of – a nonbifurcated view of reality that combines what have otherwise been divided into objective and subjective understandings, into physical and social sciences.

The nature of information systems is therefore something deeper and other than the three research approaches would have it. It is at once, rather, all *and* none of them. Information systems are in fact situated at the crux of Whitehead's bifurcation, at the nub of Bergson's quantity/quality distinction, at once both the expression and materialisation of subjective consciousness: our subjectivity made objective reality. It is, indeed, in the very meaning of the word 'information' that we will find a clue. Hayles has argued for the essential materiality of information: that it is always instantiated in some physical form – paper, screen, mechanical/electrical/photonic storage tokens. Contrary to this, early information theory, in the 1940s, 'allowed information to be conceptualised as if it were an entity that can flow unchanged between different material substrates.'[83] Even Shannon, the originator of this theory, 'did not see "too close a connection between the notion of information as we use it in communication engineering"' and the semantic questions of group communication being discussed at the eighth Macy Conference. 'He did not want to get involved in having to consider the receiver's mindset as part of the communication system.'[84] 'Information,' therefore, in the 1940s, had become conflated with 'data.' The very human, social context of 'meaning' that renders data into information – the 'receiver's mindset' – became occluded from 'information' theory in order for it to remain in keeping with positivist approaches to scientific understanding and to ensure it would be susceptible to signal processing, as I have argued elsewhere.[85]

In today's 'fourth era' IS, the use of anthropomorphic language by computing engineers must take on new meaning. As Checkland pointed out, 'Both of the pioneers von Neumann and Turing, for example, used the unjustifiable metaphor "memory" in relation to computers.' These pioneers 'could perhaps, have justified the alternative metaphor "storage."'[86] Checkland was equally critical of the use of the word 'information,' insisting that 'signal processing theory' would have been a better description. But, perhaps, acknowledging the human meaning in the word 'information' systems rather than 'data' systems, 'information systems' is indeed precisely how we ought to understand and describe them. The receiver's mind-set, in other words, is core, not only to the impact, reception, import, or use, but to the very *nature* of an 'information' system.

Information systems, in this sense, on an ontological level, are indeed closer to the 'subjective' end of the spectrum of reality than the objective, albeit bound to the motor accompaniment of computing hardware, ICT cabling, and the waveform behaviours of subatomic particles. In Whitehead's terminology, the concrescence of digital events, harvesting the influences of all the concomitant Actual Occasions of the algorithmic processing that unfolds across the space-time of photonic-token ticking around them, is a process by which we have instrumentalised rational thought; the Objective data that results are lodged within the database of the processed, ready to be looked up and used as the ongoing unfolding of the next Actual Occasion begins to concresce. This is because information systems are fundamentally embedded in social systems and are fundamentally about communication – from mind to mind and, increasingly, from autonomous systems to other autonomous systems set up like plumbing to free us from the daily trip to the well. But like sleeping policemen, for all their physicality, these autonomous systems remain messages, communications, statements within the social, means by which we establish our freedom to be other than chained to the requirements of necessity. For Bergson, it is in the manufacture of such tools, in invention per se, indeed, that the intellect distinguishes itself from instinct. This, for Bergson, is what makes the human species above the rest: 'we should say not *Homo sapiens*, but *Homo faber*,' he tells us, urging us to consider intelligence as 'the faculty of manufacturing artificial objects, especially tools to make tools, and of indefinitely varying the manufacture.'[87] In this sense IS are indeed the third great industrial revolution, and robots – which will make future information systems for us – the fourth.

Information systems, thus, carry a historicity and context as a category of human endeavour, as the critique offered in this book has shown. Rendering all information systems more human, more personal, and geared toward social good, from the logical positivist scaffold upon which they were created, is both the challenge and the task of IS researchers keen to ensure new systems are fit for purpose in today's world. IS as 'events,' in a 'structure of events,' might be considered a kind of 'infomateriality': a more durational form Orlikowski's sociomateriality, or of the 'new materialism' of Dolphijn and van der Tuin, or of a Baradian 'agential reality' specific to the meaning(s) with which we imbue the digital.[88,89] IS becomes a picture of the physicality of the hardware mediated by the data in the software into meaning in our experience, where choices are made, and thereby the data reconfigured, and the hardware driven, in cycles of mutual reinforcement.

Tech for Green Good

This book has been about the philosophy, not the practice. For the reader interested in how to put the ideas discovered in this book into operation, what advice I would give is to focus on two wings of the information systems field: ICT and sustainability, and Tech for Good, and to do so with development methodologies that incorporate human values – and the value of the planet – from the ground up.

One promising avenue in this latter field is Value Sensitive Design (VSD), which employs an iterative methodology integrating conceptual, empirical, and technical investigations. It takes quite an interactional stance toward technology and human values, in which values are sought from both direct and indirect stakeholders. It distinguishes these from designer values and seeks to explicitly support these human values with the technology it develops, in an integrative manner that involves a co-evolution of technology and social structure.[90,91] Crucially, it 'refutes the neutrality thesis of computer systems and software programs which states that such systems are in themselves neutral and depend on the user for acquiring moral status.'[92] If, as I have written elsewhere,[93] VSD can be encouraged to adopt normative positions on things, then VSD may indeed prove a useful way forward. This is work that needs to be done.

Crucially, however, one of the most important 'values' that must be embedded into VSD, into software development, information systems research, and digital transformation more broadly, is sustainability – and not just from an economic perspective, but a moral one. Sustainability is a topic that needs to be understood from an ecological rather than merely environmental perspective, but before we consider the socio-ecological sustainability of information systems, it is, of course, imperative that the hardware of the information communication technologies we use are themselves subject to major change.

A United Nations Environment Programme (UNEP) report in 2015[94] said that 'Each year, the electronic industry – one of the world's largest and fastest growing – generates up to 41 million tonnes of eWaste from goods such as computers and smart phones. Forecasts say that figure may reach 50 million tonnes already by 2017' – an alarming annual growth rate. Worse still, most of this waste is not properly recycled, but sold off illegally or simply dumped. As the report continues, 'Up to 90 per cent of the world's electronic waste, worth nearly US$19 billion, is illegally traded or dumped each year.'

But as UN Under-Secretary-General and Executive Director of UNEP Achim Steiner, said in 2014,

> Sustainable management of eWaste can combat poverty and generate green jobs through recycling, collection and processing of eWaste, and safeguard the environment and human health from the hazards posed by rising levels of waste electronics. Smart public policies, creative financial incentives and technology transfer can turn eWaste from a challenge into an important resource for sustainable development.[95]

Janez Potočnik, then European Commissioner for Environment, said in July 2014, 'It takes a tonne of ore to get one gram of gold. But you can get the same amount from recycling the materials in 41 mobile phones.'[96] In the same speech, he called for the EU to become a 'zero waste' society, with a 'circular economy' and announced a target of 70% recycling across the EU by 2030.

What are the solutions, then, and what can the information systems community do to help? Certainly, the IS community needs to press the IT industry for more recyclable electronics. A recyclable end-life for all electronic products should be part of the design, and in-built obsoleteness should be challenged. The practice of shredding, rather than disassembly, should be absolutely discouraged, as this works counter to the aims of a 'circular economy.' In short, producers and recyclers – currently living in different 'worlds' both in terms of industrial belonging, culture, status, power, etc., – need to overcome the cultural divide between 'blue chip company' and 'scrap company,' between the global nature of most producers and the local nature of most recyclers, and talk to one another. They need to reach agreements toward the creation of far more circular supply chains. Clearer information on any hazardous materials in electronics that escape such circular chains needs to be available to recyclers – for the sake of their health – and minimised in the production.

As well as the hardware change, a software change needs to get underway. A socio-ecological shift in perspective, aiming for the 'circular economy,' needs to take place. ICTs in the development context and new systems in social media need to begin to divest themselves from the yoke of neoliberalism, to prise their raison d'etre from merely increasing the bottom line, towards a more 'doughnut' economic approach which nurtures social ties, rather than seeking always to mediate them, and incorporates the value of the environment into every system.

Thankfully, elements of the business world are already ahead of the curve in this respect. Some companies are willing to stand up and challenge bad practice where it arises – such as the phenomenon of Dark UX, where some unscrupulous retailers use 'colour theory and vague micro-copy to misdirect and manipulate' visitors to their e-commerce websites, and thus 'trick customers into buying goods or signing up for services they may not have wanted.'[97] These and other practices are little better than criminal activities such as phishing.

Companies engaged in the 'Tech for Good' movement – unafraid to call out such practices – believe an ethical, moral approach to digital services and engagement is the right way forward, and are thus already a part of a wider turn toward community responsibility and an eco-social understanding of our interrelatedness. 'Tech for Good' can in many respects be seen as an outward-facing, business innovation cousin of critical information systems research – though many its many practitioners may not be aware of their friends in academia – focussed on devoting the skills of IS professionals to projects that make a positive impact in society.[98,99] Here there are carefully and cleverly worked out systems with robust coding that have been rigorously user tested with UX research techniques and are in continuous beta, constantly iterating and improving, geared towards improving people's lives in one way or another. Just two examples in the health sector are Sentimoto – 'a smartphone app that utilises existing smart watches to allow older people to access health and wellbeing information more clearly'[100]; the second is the highly topical Techfugees – 'a non-profit social enterprise co-ordinating the international tech community's response to the needs of refugees fleeing war, famine and persecution. . . . Successes include bringing wifi to the refugee camps in Calais.'[101] There are numerous other examples at the Tech for Good website (www.nptechforgood.com).

Once the inclusive process-relational approach is understood and embraced, it becomes clear that there are already a great number of projects that could be taken as examples of work that would issue from such a stance. Given the metaphysical approach outlined in this book, such work could be made even stronger, and more of it could be encouraged, and those projects that *seem* to be part of a Tech for Good movement but in reality serve the interests of neoliberal agendas become more clearly recognisable.

To summarise, this short book's core claims, as outlined in Chapter 1, have been:

- *that the early 20th-century philosophical grounding of today's digital revolution is culpable in digital's (growing) contribution to the ecological catastrophe unfolding in the 21st century*
- *that process philosophy offers a new way to rethink that philosophical grounding and reshape the digital revolution to support strategies to counter that catastrophe*

My hope is that the reader – having reached the end of this short book – can see clearly both how and why methodological individualism at the heart of positive science must be countered and what the ideas of process-relational philosophy have to offer in that attempt. In the end, there is much work to do and little time in which to achieve it. My hope is that this book will help promote at least some action in the field of information systems toward a better world, where Green Tech for Good is deployed *for* Nature, rather than against it.

Notes

1 Cohen, G.A. (1995) *Self-Ownership, Freedom and Equality*. Cambridge: Cambridge University Press, p. 20.
2 Nozick, R. (1974) *Anarchy, State and Utopia*. Oxford: Blackwell, p. 161.

3 Murphy, L., and Nagel, T. (2002) *The Myth of Ownership*. Oxford: Oxford University Press, p. 8.
4 ibid.
5 ibid.
6 Shaxson, N. (2011) *Treasure Islands: Tax Havens and the Men Who Stole the World*. London: Bodley Head.
7 Murphy, L., and Nagel, T. (2002) *The Myth of Ownership*. Oxford: Oxford University Press, p. 77.
8 ibid., p. 64.
9 ibid.
10 ibid., p. 65.
11 Rothbard, M.N. (2009) *Man, Economy, and State*. Aurburn, Alabama: Ludwig von Mises Institute.
12 Shaxson, N. (2011) *Treasure Islands: Tax Havens and the Men Who Stole the World*. London: Bodley Head.
13 Murphy, L., and Nagel, T. (2002) *The Myth of Ownership*. Oxford: Oxford University Press, p. 65.
14 Cohen, G.A. (1995) *Self-Ownership, Freedom and Equality*. Cambridge: Cambridge University Press, p. 25.
15 ibid.
16 Independent Anti-Slavery Commissioner Report, 2015–16 www.gov.uk/government/uploads/system/uploads/attachment_data/file/559571/IASC_Annual_Report_WebReadyFinal.pdf
17 Cohen, G.A. (1995) *Self-Ownership, Freedom and Equality*. Cambridge: Cambridge University Press, p. 34.
18 ibid., p. 37.
19 Mansbridge, J. (1990) 'The Rise and Fall of Self-Interest in the Explanation of Political Life' in *Beyond Self-Interest*, Mansbridge, J. (ed.), p. 20. Chicago: University of Chicago Press.
20 Sen, A.K. (1990) 'Rational Fools' in *Beyond Self-Interest*, Mansbridge, J. (ed.), p. 29. Chicago: University of Chicago Press.
21 Israel, J. (2002) *Radical Enlightenment: Philosophy and the Making of Modernity 1650–1750*. Oxford: Oxford University Press, p. 375.
22 ibid., p. 218.
23 Foucault, M. (1997) *The Order of Things*. London: Routledge.
24 Goodwin, B. (1994) *How the Leopard Changed Its Spots*. New York: Charles Scribner & Sons, p. 13.
25 Elster, J. (1990) 'Selfishness and Altruism' in *Beyond Self-Interest*, Mansbridge, J. (ed.), p. 45. Chicago: University of Chicago Press.
26 ibid.
27 Jencks, C. (1990) 'Varieties of Altruism' in *Beyond Self-Interest*, Mansbridge, J. (ed.), p. 59. Chicago: University of Chicago Press.
28 ibid., p. 3.
29 Bergson, H. (1935/2006) *The Two Sources of Morality and Religion*. Notre Dame, IN: University of Notre Dame Press, p. 14.
30 ibid., p. 30.
31 ibid., p. 32.
32 Randall, C.M. (1991) *Process Philosophy and Political Ideology*. New York: State University of New York Press, p. 5.
33 ibid., p. 7.

34 Rice, D.H. (1989) 'Critical Individualism: Whitehead's Metaphysics and Critique of Liberalism' *Journal of Value Inquiry* 23, pp. 85–97.
35 Poisson, A. (2011) 'The Influence of A.N. Whitehead on the Future of Ecological Economics' *Minding Nature* 4(1) www.humansandnature.org/the-influence-of-a.n.-whitehead-on-the-future-of-ecological-economics
36 Rodrik, D. (2017) 'The Fatal Flaw of Neoliberalism: It's Bad Economics' *The Guardian* www.theguardian.com/news/2017/nov/14/the-fatal-flaw-of-neoliberalismits-bad-economics
37 Thaler, R.H., & Sunstein, C.R. (2008) *Nudge: Improving Decisions about Health, Wealth and Happiness*. London: Penguin.
38 Raworth, K. (2017) *Doughnut Economics*. Milton Keynes: Penguin Random House, p. 127.
39 Daly, H.E. (ed.) (1973/1980) *Economics, Ecology and Ethics: Essays Toward a Steady-State Economy*. San Francisco: Freeman & Co., p. 3.
40 ibid., p. 4.
41 ibid.
42 ibid., p. 5.
43 ibid.
44 ibid., p. 8.
45 Brundtland Commission (1987) *Our Common Future* www.un-documents.net/our-common-future.pdf Para 27.
46 Daly, H.E. (ed.) (1996) *Beyond Growth*. Boston, MA: Beacon Press, p. 1.
47 Sustainable Development Goals: 17 Goals to Transform Our World www.un.org/sustainabledevelopment/sustainable-development-goals/ Department of Public Information, United Nations.
48 Rethinking Economics and the New Weather Institute (2017) *33 Theses for an Economics Reformation* www.newweather.org/wp-content/uploads/2017/12/33-Theses-for-an-Economics-Reformation.pdf
49 Mitchell, W., and Fazi, T. (2017) *Reclaiming the State: A Progressive Vision of Sovereignty for a Post-Neoliberal World*. London: Pluto Press.
50 Hutton, W. (2018) 'We Can Undo Privatisation: And It Won't Cost Us a Penny' *The Guardian* www.theguardian.com/commentisfree/2018/jan/09/nationalise-rail-gas-water-privately-owned
51 Locher, F. (2013) 'Cold War Pastures: Garrett Hardin and the "Tragedy of the Commons"' *Revue d'Histoire Moderne et Contemporaine* 60(1), pp. 7–36.
52 Locher, F. (2018) 'Debunking the Tragedy of the Commons' *CNRS News* https://news.cnrs.fr/opinions/debunking-the-tragedy-of-the-commons
53 Mirowski, P. (1991) *More Heat Than Light: Economics as Social Physics, Physics as Nature's Economics*. Cambridge, UK: Cambridge University Press.
54 Wilts, A., and White, J. (2017) 'Google, Facebook and Twitter Targeted by New Bill as Senators Seek to Stop Russian Election Meddling' *The Independent* www.independent.co.uk/news/world/americas/us-politics/google-facebook-twitter-bill-russia-election-meddling-senators-introduce-a8010056.html
55 Smith, S. (2017) 'Arm Yourself: There Is a New War, and We're Losing It' *The London Economic* www.thelondoneconomic.com/news/arm-new-war-losing/24/10/
56 Mayer, J. (2017) 'In the Withdrawal from the Paris Climate Agreement, the Koch Brothers' Campaign Becomes Overt' *The New Yorker* www.newyorker.com/news/news-desk/in-the-withdrawal-from-the-paris-climate-agreement-the-koch-brothers-campaign-becomes-overt

57 Mirowski, P. (2002) *Machine Dreams: Economics Becomes a Cyborg Science*. Cambridge: Cambridge University Press, pp. 162–176.
58 See also Beinhocker, E.D. (2007) *The Origin of Wealth: Evolution, Complexity, and the Radical Remaking of Economics*. London: Random House.
59 Raworth, K. (2017) *Doughnut Economics*. Milton Keynes: Penguin Random House, pp. 26–27.
60 Marçal, K. (2015) *Who Cooked Adam Smith's Dinner?* London: Portobello.
61 Grathwohl, C. (2017) 'Youthquake: Behind the Scenes on Selecting the Word of the Year' *Oxford Dictionaries Blog* https://blog.oxforddictionaries.com/2017/12/14/youthquake-word-of-the-year-2017-commentary/
62 Thornton, J., and Goodman, M. (2017) *Client Earth*. London: Scribe.
63 Heede, R. (2014) 'Tracing Anthropogenic Carbon Dioxide and Methane Emissions to Fossil Fuel and Cement Producers, 1854–2010' *Climate Change* 122(1–2), p. 229 https://doi.org/10.1007/s10584-013-0986-y
64 Griffin, P. (2017) The Carbon Majors Database: CDP Carbon Majors Report 2017. *Climate Accountability Institute* https://b8f65cb373b1b7b15feb-c70d8ead6ced550b4d987d7c03fcdd1d.ssl.cf3.rackcdn.com/cms/reports/documents/000/002/327/original/Carbon-Majors-Report-2017.pdf?1499691240
65 Editorial, The Guardian view on climate change: see you in court *The Guardian* www.theguardian.com/commentisfree/2017/sep/10/the-guardian-view-on-climatechange-see-you-in-court
66 Boom, K., Richards, J., and Leonard, S. (2017) Climate Justice: The International Momentum towards Climate Litigation. *Climate Justice.org* http://climatejustice.org.au/wp-content/uploads/2017/05/Report-Climate-Justice-2016.pdf
67 www.sfcityattorney.org/wp-content/uploads/2017/09/2017-09-19-File-Stamped-Complaint-for-Public-Nuisance.pdf
68 www.sfcityattorney.org/wp-content/uploads/2017/09/Oakland-file-stamped-complaint.pdf
69 Milman, O. (2018) 'New York City Plans to Divest $5bn from Fossil Fuels and Sue Oil Companies' *The Guardian* www.theguardian.com/us-news/2018/jan/10/new-york-city-plans-to-divest-5bn-from-fossil-fuels-and-sue-oil-companies
70 Lazard's Cost of Energy (2017) www.lazard.com/perspective/levelized-cost-of-energy-2017/
71 Tabi, A. (2013) 'Does Pro-Environmental Behaviour Affect Carbon Emissions?' *Energy Policy* 63, pp. 972–981.
72 Arabella Advisors (2016) The Global Fossil Fuel Divestment and Clean Energy Investment Movement www.arabellaadvisors.com/wp-content/uploads/2016/12/Global_Divestment_Report_2016.pdf
73 Doukas, A., DeAngelis, K., Ghio, N., Trout, K., and Bast, E. (2017) *Talk Is Cheap: How G20 Governments Are Financing Climate Disaster*. Oil Change International, Friends of the Earth U.S., the Sierra Club, and WWF European Policy Office http://priceofoil.org/content/uploads/2017/07/talk_is_cheap_G20_report_July2017.pdf
74 Jambeck, J., Geyer, R., Wilcox, C., Siegler, T.R., Perryman, M., Andrady, S., Narayan, R., and Law, K.L. (2015) 'Plastic Waste Inputs from Land into the Ocean' *Science* 13, pp. 768–771.
75 Austin, H.P., Allen, M.D., Donohoe, B.S., Rorrer, N.A, Kearns, F.L., Silveira, R.L., Pollard, B.C., Dominick, G., Duman, R., Omari, K.E., Mykhaylyk, V., Wagner, A., Michener, W.E., Amore, A., Skaf, M.S., Crowley, M.F., Thorne, A.W., Johnson, C.W, Woodcock, H.L., McGeehan, J.E., and Beckham, G.T. (2018). Characterization

and engineering of a plastic-degrading aromatic polyesterase. Proceedings of the National Academy of Sciences 201718804; https://doi.org/10.1073/pnas.1718804115.

76 Trash Free Seas Alliance https://oceanconservancy.org/trash-free-seas/plastics-in-the-ocean/trash-free-seas-alliance/

77 Potočnik, J. (2014) Speaking Points by Environment Commissioner Janez Potočnik on Circular Economy http://europa.eu/rapid/press-release_SPEECH-14-527_en.htm

78 Chua, W.F. (1986) 'Radical Developments in Accounting Thought' *The Accounting Review* 61, pp. 601–632.

79 Hirschheim, R., and Klein, H. (2012) 'A Glorious and Not-So-Short History of the Information Systems Field' *Journal of the Association for Information Systems* 13(4), p. 215.

80 Evans, J. (2010) 'Here Comes the Wetware' *TechCrunch* https://techcrunch.com/2010/12/04/wetware/

81 Moore, P., and Robinson, A. (2015) 'The Quantified Self: What Counts in the Neoliberal Workplace' *New Media & Society* 18(11), pp. 2774–2792.

82 Parry, R. (2014) 'Episteme and Techne' in *The Stanford Encyclopedia of Philosophy*, Zalta, E.N. (ed.) https://plato.stanford.edu/archives/fall2014/entries/episteme-techne/

83 Hayles, N.K. (1999) *How We Became Postmodern*. Chicago: University of Chicago Press, p. 1.

84 ibid., p. 54.

85 Kreps, D. (2017) 'Matter and Memory and Deep Learning' in *Berukuson* Busshitsu to Kioku *wo Shindan suru: Jikan Keiken no Tetsugaku, Ishiki no Kagaku, Bigaku, Rinrigaku eno Tenkai* (*Diagnoses of Bergson's* Matter and Memory: *Developments Towards the Philosophy of Temporal Experience, Sciences of Consciousness, Aesthetics, and Ethics*), Hirai, Y., Fujita, H., and Abiko, S. (eds.), pp 196–225. Tokyo: Shoshi Shinsui.

86 Checkland, P. (1988) 'Information Systems and Systems Thinking: Time to Unite?' *International Journal of Information Management* 8, p. 239.

87 Bergson, H. (1907/1944) *Creative Evolution*. Translated by A. Mitchell, with a Foreword by I. Edman. New York: Random House Modern Library.

88 Barad, K. (2007) *Meeting the Universe Halfway*. London: Duke University Press.

89 Orlikowski, W. (2005) 'Material Works: Exploring the Situated Entanglement of Technological Performativity and Human Agency' *Scandinavian Journal of Information Systems* 17(1), pp. 183–186.

90 Friedman, B., Kahn, P.H., Jr., and Borning, A. (2006) 'Value Sensitive Design and Information Systems' in *Human-Computer Interaction in Management Information Systems: Foundations*, Zhang, P. and Galletta, D. (eds.), pp. 348–372. Armonk, NY: M. E. Sharpe.

91 Davis, J., & Nathan, L.P. (2014) 'Value Sensitive Design: Applications, Adaptations, and Critiques' in *Ethics and Values in Technological Design*, van de Poel, I., Vermaas, P., and van den Hoven, J. (eds.). Heidelberg: Springer Reference Works.

92 van Wynsberghe, A. (2013) 'Designing Robots for Care: Care Centered Value-Sensitive Design' *Science and Engineering Ethics* 19(2), pp. 407–433.

93 Kreps, D., and Burmeister, O.K. (2017) 'I Am a Person: A Review of Value Sensitive Design for Cognitive Declines of Ageing, Interpreted through the

Lens of Personhood' *Paper presented at ETHICOMP 2017*. Turin, Italy, 5–8 June.

94 Rucevska, I., Nellemann, C., Isarin, N., Yang, W., Liu, N., Yu, K., Sandnæs, S., Olley, K., McCann, H., Devia, L., Bisschop, L., Soesilo, D., Schoolmeester, T., Henriksen, R., and Nilsen, R. (2015) *Waste Crime–Waste Risks: Gaps in Meeting the Global Waste Challenge*. A UNEP Rapid Response Assessment. Nairobi and Arendal: United Nations Environment Programme and GRID-Arendal www.grida.no

95 www.unenvironment.org/news-and-stories/press-release/conference-spotlight-new-e-waste-management-solutions-kenya accessed 21.12.2017.

96 http://europa.eu/rapid/press-release_SPEECH-14-527_en.htm accessed 21.12.2017.

97 www.wearesigma.com/cxmas/index.html

98 Tech For Good (2016) www.techforgood.global accessed 12.8.2016.

99 Hull, R., and Berry, R. (2016) 'The Social Entrepreneurship Option for Scientists and Engineers' in *Engineering and Enterprise: Inspiring Innovation*, Bhamidimarri, R. and Liu, A. (eds.). Switzerland: Springer.

100 Firman, S. (15 July 2016) www.techforgood.global/blog/nestas-tech-for-good-new-radicals-of-2016/ accessed 12.8.2016.

101 ibid.

Index

For Product Safety Concerns and Information please contact our EU representative GPSR@taylorandfrancis.com
Taylor & Francis Verlag GmbH, Kaufingerstraße 24, 80331 München, Germany

www.ingramcontent.com/pod-product-compliance
Ingram Content Group UK Ltd.
Pitfield, Milton Keynes, MK11 3LW, UK
UKHW021421080625
459435UK00011B/99

* 9 7 8 0 3 6 7 6 0 7 0 1 2 *